Implementing Regulatory Impact Analysis in the Central Government of Peru

CASE STUDIES 2014-16

OECD
BETTER POLICIES FOR BETTER LIVES

Please cite this publication as:
OECD (2019), *Implementing Regulatory Impact Analysis in the Central Government of Peru: Case Studies 2014-16*, OECD Publishing, Paris, *https://doi.org/10.1787/9789264305786-en*.

ISBN 978-92-64-30577-9 (print)
ISBN 978-92-64-30578-6 (pdf)

Photo credits: Cover © Natali Eki/Shutterstock.com.

Corrigenda to OECD publications may be found on line at: *www.oecd.org/about/publishing/corrigenda.htm*.

Foreword

As noted in the *2012 OECD Recommendation of the Council on Regulatory Policy and Governance*, every government should seek to establish a regulatory framework that contains quality regulations, which achieve legitimate public policy objectives without imposing unnecessary costs on business and citizens.

The *Recommendation* provides governments with clear and timely guidance on the principles, mechanisms, and institutions needed to improve the design, implementation and review of their regulatory frameworks, with a focus on the highest standards. One of the main mechanisms promoted by the *Recommendation* is a system for the *ex ante* evaluation of prospective regulations, in order to ensure their quality.

Quality regulations can foster innovation, facilitate entry into new markets, promote the adoption of international standards, and enhance competition; at the same time, they can help achieve societal objectives such as protecting the environment, consumers, and workers. All this contributes to increased productivity and inclusive growth.

The report identifies the legal and institutional framework, and the processes followed in Peru to issue regulations in the period 2014-16. It evaluates those elements taking as reference the most relevant practices of the regulatory impact assessment system in OECD countries. It offers recommendations to help Peru step up its efforts to enhance the quality of its regulations and thus contribute to improving economic growth and social development in the country.

This report also monitors the implementation of the findings and recommendations from the *2016 OECD Review of Regulatory Policy in Peru: Assembling the Framework for Regulatory Quality,* which suggested that Peru should introduce a system of regulatory impact assessment for draft regulations and regulations that are subject to modifications, as part of its administrative procedures.

Acknowledgements

The country reviews on regulatory reform are co-ordinated by the Directorate for Public Governance, under the responsibility of Marcos Bonturi, and are carried out by the Regulatory Policy Division, headed by Nick Malyshev.

The review would have not been possible without the support of the government of Peru. The OECD Secretariat is grateful to the Carlos Augusto Oliva Neyra, Minister of Economy and Finance. The review team would like to thank in particular Pedro Herrera, General Director of International Economy, Competition, and Productivity Affairs within that Ministry. Additionally, to Miguel Ángel Luque, Miguel Figallo, Daniela Britto, then at the Ministry of Economy and Finance and José Alfredo la Rosa, for their unique assistance in collecting data and information, organising the team's fact-finding missions, and providing feedback throughout the development of the review.

Officials of the central government provided valuable contributions, including the Ministry of Economy and Finance, the Presidency of the Council of Ministers, the Ministry of Justice and Human Rights, the Ministry of Environment, the Ministry of Production, the Ministry of Transport and Communications, and the Ministry of Housing, Construction and Sanitation.

This report includes the inputs and feedback from peers of country members of the OECD Regulatory Policy Committee.

Manuel Gerardo Flores, Senior Economist of the OECD Regulatory Policy Division, managed the project. The following team members took primary responsibility for different sections of the Review: Andrés Blancas, Adriana García, Gloriana Madrigal, Alberto Morales, Delia Vázquez, and Manuel Gerardo Flores. Erik Pérez helped with the research. Celine Kauffmann and Andrea Uhrhammer provided feedback to improve drafts of the report. Claudia Paupe and Mariama Diallo provided administrative assistance, and Jennifer Stein co-ordinated the editorial process. Erik Perez and Gloriana Madrigal helped with the English version of the report.

Table of contents

Tables

Figures

Boxes

Follow OECD Publications on:

http://twitter.com/OECD_Pubs

http://www.facebook.com/OECDPublications

http://www.linkedin.com/groups/OECD-Publications-4645871

http://www.youtube.com/oecdilibrary

OECD Alerts http://www.oecd.org/oecddirect/

Abbreviations and acronyms

CBA	Cost-benefit analysis
CCR	Multisectoral Commission of Regulatory Quality
CCV	Vice-Ministerial Coordinating Council
CEA	Cost-Effectiveness Analysis
COFEMER	Federal Commission for Regulatory Improvement
CONAMER	National Commission for Regulatory Improvement
FOG	Federal Official Gazette
INDECOPI	National Institute for the Defense of Free Competition and Protection of Intellectual Property
MEF	Ministry of Economy and Finance
MINAM	Ministry of Environment
MINJUSDH	Ministry of Justice and Human Rights
MIR	Regulatory Impact Expression
MTC	Ministry of Transport and Communications
OECD	Organisation for Economic Co-operation and Development
PCM	Presidency of the Council of Ministers
PIDE	State Interoperability Platform
PRODUCE	Ministry of Production
RCC	Regulatory Criteria Checklist
RIA	Regulatory impact assessment
RIS	Regulatory impact statement
RQA	Regulatory Quality Analysis
SMART	Specific, Measurable, Achievable, Realistic, Timely
VIVIENDA	Ministry of Housing, Construction and Sanitation

Executive summary

Regulations can have a positive or negative impact on the performance of an economic sector or economy. A specific regulation can open or close markets, can promote the elimination or creation of monopolies, can raise entry barriers, or can reduce or boost incentives for innovation or entrepreneurship. It is therefore important to review and improve the process of issuing regulations, to ensure that they are fit-for-purpose, that they will effectively address the policy problems that gave rise to them, and that their goals contribute to social welfare and inclusive growth.

This review looks at how the use of regulatory impact assessment (RIA) can help make the process for issuing regulations in the central government of Peru more efficient and effective. RIA helps improve the decision-making process that defines the rules. It also makes the agency issuing regulations aware both of the problem that needs to be addressed, and of the different ways to solve it. In addition, RIA considers the financial sustainability of implementing a regulation or, in other words, whether its costs will be lower than its benefits. RIA thus provides a method of analysis based on evidence and empirical information that helps improve the quality of rules issued.

This review documents and evaluates the process followed by the following five ministries to issue regulations during the 2014-16 period, and compares it to the most relevant RIA practices in OECD countries:

- Ministry of Economy and Finance
- Ministry of Environment
- Ministry of Production
- Ministry of Transport and Communications
- Ministry of Housing, Construction and Sanitation

It also looks at the legal and institutional framework put in place by Peru to issue regulations and evaluate them *ex ante*. OECD recommendations regarding RIA form the baseline for the review.

Main findings

- In recent years, the Peruvian government has implemented a series of measures to improve the quality of regulations. However, within the public administration there is no horizontal policy for the adoption of an *ex ante* evaluation system that assesses impact and regulatory quality.
- An important step is the recent creation of the Regulatory Quality Analysis system, which creates an *ex ante* evaluation system of the administrative procedures for drafting regulations. Its implementation means the first systematised process in the Government of Peru to evaluate the impacts of new rules. By focusing only on administrative procedures, the scope of the Regulatory Quality Analysis does not

match that of an AIR system, in which the regulations are comprehensively evaluated.

- The recent creation of a committee composed of the Ministry of Economy and Finance, the Presidency of the Council of Ministers, and the Ministry of Justice and Human Rights, in charge of a pilot programme of *ex ante* evaluation through simplified RIA, is promising. The committee, however, has no legal basis, and has not produced any guidance for ministries or government agencies on carrying out RIA.
- Within the five selected ministries, the process for issuing regulations is virtually the same. The most important exception was identified in the Ministry of Environment, which carries out a deeper consultation process that observes good RIA practices.
- The process to issue regulations is not standardised, because it does not have a specific regulatory policy instrument that supports it.
- It is evident that within this process there is no formalised oversight or accountability regarding the way in which a regulation is issued, at least from a whole-of-government approach.
- Initial efforts have been made to carry out a cost-benefit evaluation of regulations, but much remains to be done to systematise and improve the quality of the exercise.
- Public consultation on proposed regulations is used only intermittently. Moreover, there is no legal obligation to reply to public comments, nor to show that the proposal was modified as a result of the consultation.
- The activities carried out by the Ministry of Environment during the consultation are the exception, and include creating a matrix of comments, meetings with the public, and redrafting the regulatory proposal.

Main recommendations

- Establish a binding legal instrument stating the obligation for ministries and government agencies to carry out an *ex ante* evaluation of regulatory proposals, and make public consultation an essential element. The issuance of Legislative Decree 1448 is an encouraging development in this direction because it establishes as an instrument of regulatory quality the analysis of *ex ante* and *ex post* regulatory impact.
- Give legal status to the committee comprised of the Presidency of the Council of Ministers, the Ministry of Economy and Finance and the Ministry of Justice and Human Rights in charge of the simplified RIA pilot programme.
- Define a list and/or criteria for those regulatory proposals that will be exempted from RIA because they do not have any impact on regulated parties.
- Issue guidance on the simplified RIA currently used in the pilot programme.
- Consider establishing an oversight body that concentrates most, if not all, of the regulatory policy activities and tools currently spread across several ministries, agencies, and offices. This oversight body should have legal capability and the necessary resources to carry out an active enforcement of activities, while

overseeing overall regulatory policy, including the authority to return draft regulation when the defined criteria are not met.

- Issue an RIA manual, which includes a standardised process for the consultation stage of the regulatory proposal with the following characteristics:
  - The regulatory proposal and the corresponding RIA should be made available for consultation by the public for a minimum of 30 business days.
  - Regulated parties should be able to comment on both the regulatory proposal and the RIA.
  - Ministries and agencies that issue regulations must reply to all the comments and, at the end of the process, issue a document summarising all comments received and the actions that will be taken to address the relevant ones.
- Establish at least two types of RIA, one for high-impact regulatory proposals, for which a thorough and in-depth impact analysis must be carried out; and another, less substantial, analysis for the remaining proposals. In this report, model processes are suggested for the issuance of regulations according to the type of RIA

Chapter 1. Regulatory impact assessment within the regulatory governance cycle

This chapter describes the relevance and need of evaluating the quality of regulations. It also introduces regulatory impact assessment, a tool used in several OECD countries for analysing the quality of regulations and implementing the best draft proposals that lead to net benefits for society. Moreover, it explains the link between regulatory impact assessment and the regulatory governance cycle.

The importance of evaluating draft regulations[1] lies in the potential effects they may produce, either positive or negative. Ideally, regulatory proposals that are intended to be implemented must produce not only positive net benefits, but also the greatest possible benefit. This task implies the application of an evaluation process of the regulation that examines its design, selects the best alternative to solve the problem, and that identifies what are the benefits for society.

The need to assess regulation

Regulation is the set of rules of law from different hierarchical levels that defines the participation of people or companies in a market, a sector, or in some economic or social activity. The process by which these rules are established and enforced may define its relevance, importance, and effect on the subject and the purpose of the legislation. This implies that the process to issue regulations determines its quality, and it has a direct impact on the results or consequences of public policy.

It is important to emphasise this aspect, the quality in the process to issue regulations has a direct impact on the expected results once it is enacted (even, it often produces effects that were not identified). This means that the process to issue regulations has significant influence on the accomplishment of the stated goals and the possible net potential benefit; these and other aspects are discussed below.

In fact, specific rules can open or close markets, can promote the elimination or creation of monopolies, can produce entry barriers, can reduce or boost the incentives for innovation or entrepreneurship, and so forth. It can also ensure the quality of public services, such as education, health, etcetera. It is very important to review and improve the process followed to issue regulation, to ensure that it is rightly oriented, and it is aimed to address a specific problem.

The OECD, through the Regulatory Policy Committee, published the Recommendations of the Council on Regulatory Policy and Governance (OECD, 2012[1]). These recommendations explicitly emphasise the importance of implementing a process that monitors the quality of regulations (see Box 1.1).

For example, the first recommendation of the Council states the commitment at the highest political level of an explicit whole-of-government policy to monitor the quality of regulations. The second recommendation refers to the principles of open government, including the participation of stakeholders in the regulatory process, and the development of comprehensible and clear regulations. The fourth recommendation focuses on the Regulatory Impact Assessment (RIA), a specific tool to evaluate the possible effects of rules (OECD, 2012[1]).

The work performed by the OECD on regulatory policy has produced several documents, including those identifying the possible positive effects of a public policy of this nature. For instance, growth and economic development have been promoted through a policy that includes structural reforms, liberalisation of markets, opening of markets, and the creation of a non-very restrictive setting for business (OECD, 2014[2]). Furthermore, the link between the regulatory policy and a series of structural reforms is recognised, out of which the following ones have been documented:

- The reciprocal relationship between an effective regulatory policy and the opening of markets, which in consequence opens channels for innovation, entrepreneurship, and strengthens the benefits for consumers.

- The relationship between the principles of competition policy and those that promote the quality of regulation.
- The relationship between the reform of regulated markets and infrastructure, and the positive effects on price reduction, innovation, quality of service, and consumer choice.

Box 1.1. Recommendation of the Council on Regulatory Policy and Governance

1. Commit at the highest political level to an explicit whole-of-government policy for regulatory quality. The policy should have clear objectives and frameworks for implementation to ensure that, if regulation is used, the economic, social and environmental benefits justify the costs, the distributional effects are considered and the net benefits are maximised.
2. Adhere to principles of open government, including transparency and participation in the regulatory process to ensure that regulation serves the public interest and is informed by the legitimate needs of those interested in and affected by regulation. This includes providing meaningful opportunities (including online) for the public to contribute to the process of preparing draft regulatory proposals and to the quality of the supporting analysis. Governments should ensure that regulations are comprehensible and clear and that parties can easily understand their rights and obligations.
3. Establish mechanisms and institutions to actively provide oversight of regulatory policy procedures and goals, support and implement regulatory policy, and thereby foster regulatory quality.
4. Integrate Regulatory Impact Assessment (RIA) into the early stages of the policy process for the formulation of new regulatory proposals. Clearly identify policy goals and evaluate if regulation is necessary and how it can be most effective and efficient in achieving those goals. Consider means other than regulation and identify the tradeoffs of the different approaches analysed to identify the best approach.
5. Conduct systematic programme reviews of the stock of significant regulation against clearly defined policy goals, including consideration of costs and benefits, to ensure that regulations remain up to date, cost justified, cost effective and consistent, and deliver the intended policy objectives.
6. Regularly publish reports on the performance of regulatory policy and reform programmes, and the public authorities applying the regulations. Such reports should also include information on how regulatory tools such as Regulatory Impact Assessment (RIA), public consultation practices, and reviews of existing regulations are functioning in practice.
7. Develop a consistent policy covering the role and functions of regulatory agencies in order to provide greater confidence that regulatory decisions are made on an objective, impartial and consistent basis, without conflict of interest, bias or improper influence.

8. Ensure the effectiveness of systems for the review of the legality and procedural fairness of regulations and of decisions made by bodies empowered to issue regulatory sanctions. Ensure that citizens and businesses have access to these systems of review at reasonable cost and receive decisions in a timely manner.
9. As appropriate, apply risk assessment, risk management, and risk communication strategies to the design and implementation of regulations to ensure that regulation is targeted and effective. Regulators should assess how regulations will be given effect and should design responsive implementation and enforcement strategies.
10. Where appropriate, promote regulatory coherence through co-ordination mechanisms between the supranational, the national, and sub-national levels of government. Identify cross-cutting regulatory issues at all levels of government, to promote coherence between regulatory approaches and avoid duplication or conflict of regulations.
11. Foster the development of regulatory management capacity and performance at sub-national levels of government.
12. In developing regulatory measures, give consideration to all relevant international standards and frameworks for co-operation in the same field and, where appropriate, their likely effects on parties outside the jurisdiction.

Source: (OECD, 2012[1]), *Recommendation of the Council on Regulatory Policy and Governance*, Paris, https://doi.org/10.1787/9789264209022-en.

Currently, many countries have adopted a regulatory policy; however, there are important challenges in terms of regulation. For example; the lack of consistency and continuity in the implementation of regulation; the promotion of the participation of diverse actors interested in the regulatory process; the capability to implement an effective regulation, as well as the limited process to evaluate regulation. For these reasons, it is important to promote a regulatory policy programme that includes goals as the following ones (OECD, 2015[3]):

- Reducing the perverse and unintended effects of regulation;
- Reducing regulatory burdens by deregulating and the alternatives to the regulation;
- Reducing inconsistencies in regulation and the lack of experience, and
- Reducing the lack of institutional capacity and professionalisation in regulation.

As rules can have a positive or negative impact on the performance of an economic sector, an economic or social activity, it is urgent to conclude that it is necessary to study the process for the issuance of regulations to ensure that there are criteria guaranteeing their contribution to social welfare, that expected goals are achieved, and that the potential risks which gave rise to the regulations are reduced. One of the most widely used instruments to achieve this goal among OECD countries is the Regulatory Impact Assessment (RIA), a tool that enables to assess if the proposed regulation is the best option (whether regulatory or not) and if the net benefit is positive. In this way, the risk of designing and implementing draft proposals that have not been assessed is reduced.

Essential building blocks of RIA: introduction

The Regulatory Impact Assessment (RIA) is a tool that consistently examines the benefits, costs and potential effects of a draft regulation (or non-regulatory alternative), either a new one or the modification of a preexisting one. This tool is a diffused practice through virtually all OECD countries, as an instrument to monitor and ensure the effectiveness of regulation. In practice, all OECD countries use a version of RIA to analyse their regulation (see next section which provides a summarised description of RIA practices in OECD countries;, see also, Chapter 2 which presents a more thorough description of the RIA system in some OECD countries). Box 1.2 offers an example of the adoption of the regulatory impact assessment tool, particularly in the United States.

Box 1.2. The RIA model in the United States

The main reasons that led to the introduction of RIA in the United States were: i) the need to ensure that federal agencies justify regulatory interventions before issuing a regulation, and consider lighter interventions before committing to a heavy regulation; ii) the need of the central government of controlling the conduct of agencies, upon which regulatory powers were conferred; and iii) the need to promote the efficiency of regulatory decisions by introducing the obligation of carrying out a cost-benefit analysis in the RIA.

Underlying the introduction of RIA, from a general point of view, was the idea that policy makers should make informed decisions, based on all available evidence. In the case of the United States, this idea was initially associated with a clear emphasis on the need to avoid imposing unnecessary regulatory burdens on business, a result that —on principle— was guaranteed by introducing the general obligation of performing a cost-benefit analysis of the alternatives to the regulation and justify the adoption of such regulation with net benefits. Although the US system has remained almost unchanged, the initial approach was partially modified: from cost reduction to a better balance between the benefits and regulatory costs.

The first steps of the RIA included a reform of the governance arrangements adopted by the administration to develop draft proposals.

- RIA was introduced as a mandatory procedure within an existing set of administrative rules.
- The introduction of RIA required the creation of a central oversight body in charge of evaluating the quality of the RIAs produced, the Office of Information and Regulatory Affairs.
- A focus on cost-benefit analysis. The RIA system in the United States is clearly and explicitly based on the practice of the cost-benefit analysis.

Source: (OECD, 2015[4]), *Regulatory Policy in Perspective: A Reader's Companion to the OECD Regulatory Policy Outlook 2015*, Paris, https://doi.org/10.1787/9789264241800-en.

One of the main reasons for the widespread dissemination of RIA is that it helps to improve the decision-making process that defines the regulation. Regulatory impact assessment promotes a systematic process, with a comparative approach on policy decisions (OECD, 2008[5]), and it makes the agency issuing regulations aware of the accurate identification of the problem that needs to be addressed, as well as of the different alternatives to achieve it.

Additionally, RIA asks about the financial sustainability of implementing a regulation or, in other words, that its costs be lower than the benefits.

Another advantage of RIA is that it provides a method of analysis based on evidence and empirical information that compares different proposals or alternatives, it promotes the identification of benefits and costs (direct or indirect) derived from the regulation, it establishes a rational decision-making system, and evaluates regulation on a cross-cutting basis, etcetera. Table 1.1 shows the essential stages of RIA which, if correctly addressed, will translate into an effective evaluation of the quality of regulation (Chapter 5 includes the assessment of each one of these stages in the process to issue regulations in Peru).

The *ex ante* evaluation provided by the RIA should ideally include an analysis of the need to regulate or, even, of government intervention through the identification of a specific problem, such as market failures, asymmetry of information, the need to protect citizen rights, and so forth (definition of the problem). This analysis produces not only a clear and concise identification of the problem but the best option for government intervention, if it is justifiable (public policy objective); which can be a regulatory instrument or another of different sort (alternatives to the regulation).

Table 1.1. Essential building blocks of RIA

Building block
Definition of the problem
Public policy objectives
Alternatives to the regulation
Impact evaluation
Compliance with regulation
Monitoring and evaluation
Public consultation

During the decision-making process, regarding the alternative of government intervention (which may be regulatory or non-regulatory), officials should:

- Assess the economic, social and environmental impacts, considering the possible special and long-term effects;
- Evaluate if the adoption of international instruments can reduce the public policy problems that have been identified and promote coherence at global level, with minimum alteration of domestic and international markets,
- This analysis always must consider, as an alternative, the option of not acting at all, which will be the baseline for the comparative analysis.

The impact evaluation aims to identify the costs and benefits of regulation, whether direct or indirect, for later quantification if possible. The impact evaluation can be considered as the core of RIA, because the main role of this tool is to understand the impact that regulation may have on individuals, industry, and the government itself. According to the OECD Recommendation, in the case of draft proposals with potentially important impacts on society, the *ex ante* analysis of the proposals should preferably be quantitative. This evaluation should include direct (administrative, financial, etcetera) and indirect costs (opportunity costs or spillover effects).

However, the mere fact of identifying costs and benefits in a qualitative manner is an important step that can help to improve the process. In any case, it is important to make a qualitative description of the costs and benefits identified, before their quantification (if this is possible).

The evaluation of public policy must consider the strategies and resources necessary to ensure the compliance with regulation. In order to achieve the objective that has been set out, it is necessary to ensure that regulated parties meet the obligations that are intended to be established. The monitoring and evaluation of the draft proposal will make it possible to clearly identify if the public policy objectives are being reached, as well as to determine if the proposed regulation is needed, or how can it be more effective and efficient to achieve the stated objectives.

The results of the evaluation exercise (RIA) should be made available to the public along with the regulatory proposal, in order to receive comments from the interested parties and, based on that, to develop a second and improved draft of the proposal (public consultation), if applicable. According to the Recommendation of the Council, carrying out the public consultation as part of the RIA process is a good practice.

In addition to the essential RIA stages, a condition for the proper development of the evaluation process is that it must be monitored by an entity that has as one of its key objectives to ensure that the process of issuing regulations goes beyond the controls designed with defined standards (oversight body). This process should clearly identify the priorities, risks, exceptions, and impact (see Recommendation 3 in (OECD, 2012[1]). The tasks of such entity normally go beyond those related with the Regulatory Impact Assessment; if possible, they should include the entire cycle of regulatory governance. Table 1.2 shows the tasks of the supervisory agencies of regulatory policy.

Table 1.2. The functions of oversight bodies

Areas of responsibility	Functions	Location
Consultation/stakeholder engagement	**Quality assurance**	**Within government**
Legal quality	• Scrutinise evaluations	• Centre of government (e.g. PMs office, cabinet office)
Administrative simplification	• Challenge unsatisfactory tools or processes	• Ministry of Finance / Ministry of Economy / Treasury
RIA	• Review legal quality	• Ministry of Justice
Ex post evaluation	**Identifying areas of policy where regulation can be more effective**	• Other ministries
Other (e.g. de-regulation agenda or e government)	• Gather opinions from stakeholders on areas in which regulatory costs are excessive and submit them to individual departments/ministries	**External to government**
	• Reviews of existing regulation	• Independent bodies
	• Analysis of stock and/or flow of regulation	• Parliament
	• Advocate for particular areas of reform	• Advisory group
	Systematic improvement of regulatory policy	• Office of Attorney General
	• Institutional relations, e.g. co-operation with international for a	
	• Co-ordination with other oversight bodies	
	• Monitoring and reporting, including report progress to parliament/government to help track success of implementation of regulatory policy	

Areas of responsibility	Functions	Location
	Co-ordination of regulatory tools • Encourage the smooth adoption of the different aspects of regulatory policy at every stage of the policy cycle **Guidance and training** • Issue guidelines • Prove assistance and advice to regulators for performing assessments	

Source: Based on (OECD, 2012[1]), *Recommendation of the Council on Regulatory Policy and Governance*, Paris, https://dx.doi.org/10.1787/9789264209022-en; Renda, A. (2015), "Regulatory Impact Assessment and Regulatory Policy" in (OECD, 2015[4]), *Regulatory Policy in Perspective: A Reader's Companion to the OECD Regulatory Policy Outlook 2015*, Paris; and OECD 2014 Regulatory Indicators Survey results, www.oecd.org/gov/regulatory-policy/measuringregulatory-performance.htm.

The international practice of the RIA

Regulatory impact assessment is a tool that, ideally, should be applied to primary and subordinate laws; otherwise, the quality that is earned in a segment can be undermined by its subordinate regulations. Figure 1.1 includes a composite indicator showing the level of adoption of the RIA. This means, the formal requirements provided for in the regulatory framework to implement this tool, including institutional arrangement. It also includes the methodology used, that is, how the impacts of regulation are assessed, considering the costs and benefits, the regulatory and non-regulatory alternatives, the risks assessment, as well as the existence of a guide for the application of the methodology defined. The third component of the indicator considers the supervision throughout the process, which implies having tasks formally established to oversee the RIA practice and requirements in place to ensure the quality of the analysis of the regulation, and transparency among the OECD countries. The former is understood as the capability of the RIA process to open itself to interested parties and the extent to which they can participate in it. As it can be confirmed, the United Kingdom, Mexico, and the European Union are the ones with the most outstanding practices for primary laws.

Figure 1.2 shows the same indicator for subordinate laws. At this hierarchical level, the United Kingdom, Mexico, and the European Union countries continue as the ones with the highest score in the application of the methodology, the transparency process, the adoption and supervision of the RIA. It is important to mention that in those countries the practice of implementing RIA stands out, according to their principles and legal framework. It does not imply, however, that there are not several areas for improvement in the application of these systems, since one of the main challenges within the regulatory quality processes is, precisely, their implementation.

The OECD has closely monitored the work performed in Latin America regarding the development and application of RIA, particularly in countries such as Brazil, Chile, Colombia, Costa Rica, Ecuador, Mexico, and Peru. In this region, the use of RIA is being more common, but the dissemination of this tool still requires a significant boost. In Latin America, only three countries have the formal requirement of conducting RIA; in two of them it was formalised for all subordinate regulations, and in one of them for a subset of the regulation (Querbach and Arndt, 2017[6]). Nevertheless, RIA is applied in four countries; in one of them to all the regulation, and in the other three to a subset. This implies that, at least, there is one country lagging in the use of the RIA although it is a formal requirement and one country uses this practice without included it in legal instruments (see Figure 1.3).

Figure 1.1. Composite indicators: regulatory impact assessment for developing primary laws

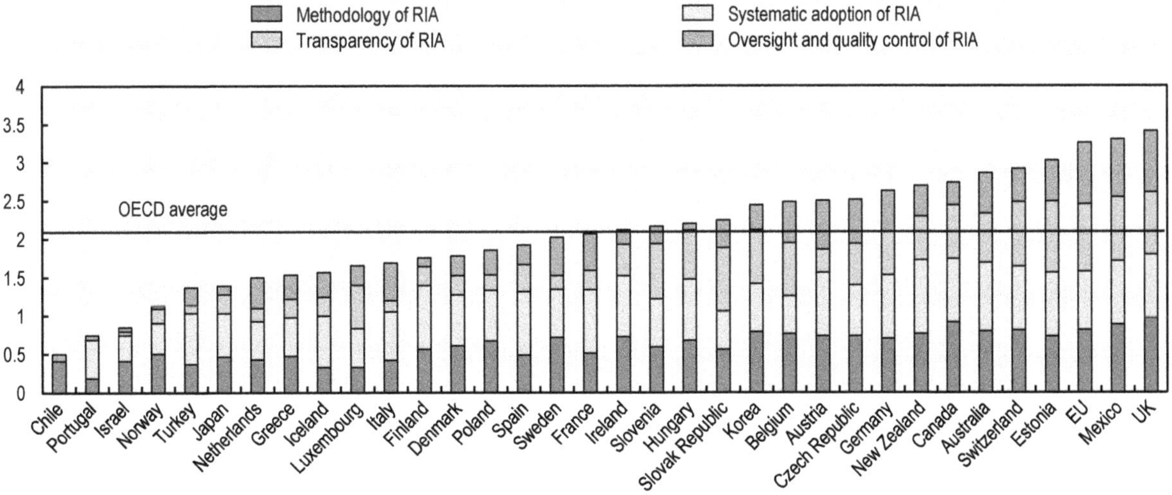

Notes: The results apply only to processes for the development of primary laws initiated by the Executive. The vertical axis represents the total aggregate score across the four separate categories of the composite indicators. The maximum score for each category is one, and the maximum aggregate score for the indicator is four. The figure excludes the United States, where all primary laws are initiated by Congress. In most countries, almost all primary laws are initiated by the Executive, with the exception of Mexico and Korea, where a large part of them is initiated by Parliament / Congress (90.6% and 84%, respectively).

Source: OECD 2014 Regulatory Indicators Survey results, www.oecd.org/gov/regulatory-policy/measuring-regulatory-performance.htm.

Figure 1.2. Composite indicators: regulatory impact assessment for developing subordinate laws

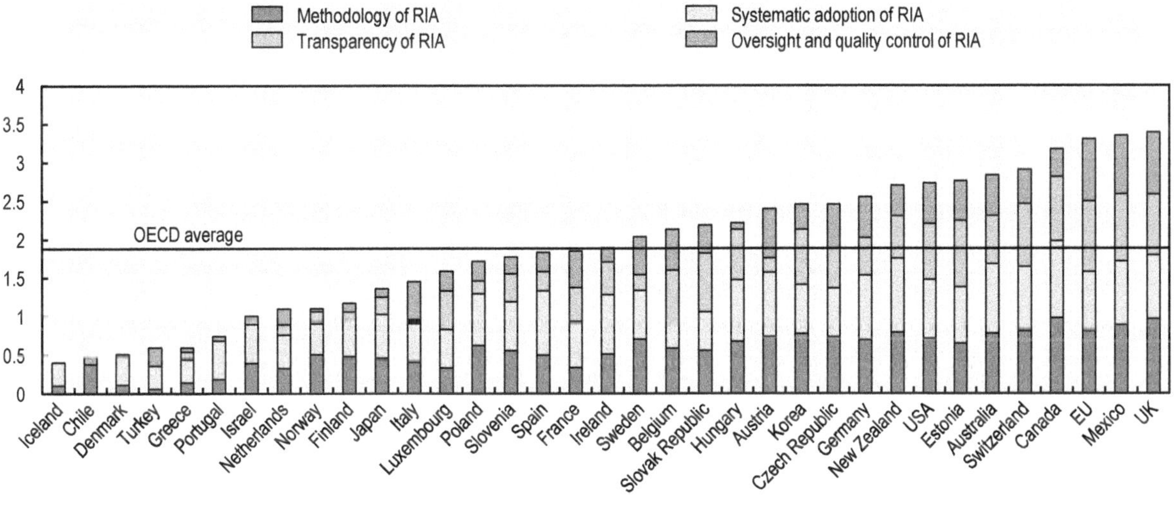

Notes. The vertical axis represents the total aggregate score across the four separate categories of the composite indicator. The maximum score for each category is one, and the maximum aggregate score for the indicator is four.

Source: OECD 2014 Regulatory Indicators Survey results, www.oecd.org/gov/regulatory-policy/measuring-regulatory-performance.htm.

Figure 1.3. The adoption of RIA: formal requirements and practices in Latin America

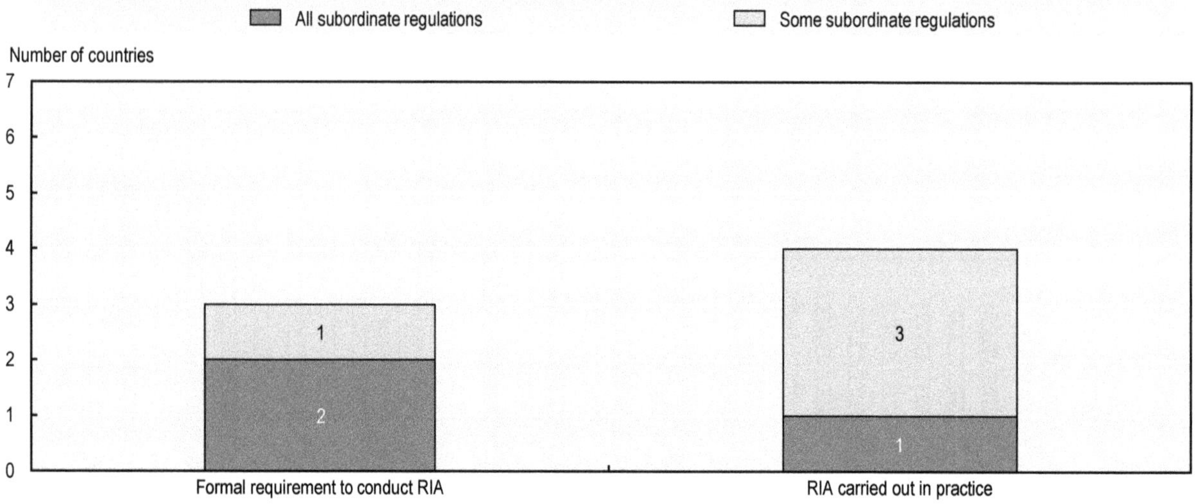

Source: (Querbach and Arndt, 2017[6]), "Regulatory policy in Latin America: An analysis of the state of play", *OECD Regulatory Policy Working Papers*, No. 7, Paris, http://dx.doi.org/10.1787/2cb29d8c-en.

Among the countries where a RIA is conducted, Mexico is probably the best example, because it was implemented for all subordinate regulation originated in the Executive. Costa Rica has enforced RIA, but only for the regulation that creates formalities. Finally, Brazil has different public entities with an important degree of independence that have adopted RIA, but it is not a cross-cutting practice within the government.

RIA as an element of the regulatory governance cycle

The goals of a regulatory policy programme are part of a broader process that includes RIA. For instance, there are additional elements to ensure the quality of regulations such as the public consultation and the regulatory impact assessment. Taken together, these tools are key elements of, what the OECD calls, the regulatory governance cycle, which is the model that it uses to ensure the effectiveness of regulation (see Figure 1.4). In fact, among the most important recommendations from the OECD in this regards, is the adoption of the complete cycle, under an approach based on evidence and risk identification.

According to the OECD, it is important to adopt a method of assessing regulations during the design stages (*ex ante*), that considers proportionality and cost-benefit criteria. Therefore, RIA is a key element for a proper management of the regulatory governance cycle. In fact, a relevant practice as to regulatory governance – and considered necessary to achieve the results planned in the public policies designed – involves a process of cyclical analysis that links the conception of the regulation with its performance, once it is enforced and produces its first effects.

Figure 1.4. Cycle of regulatory governance

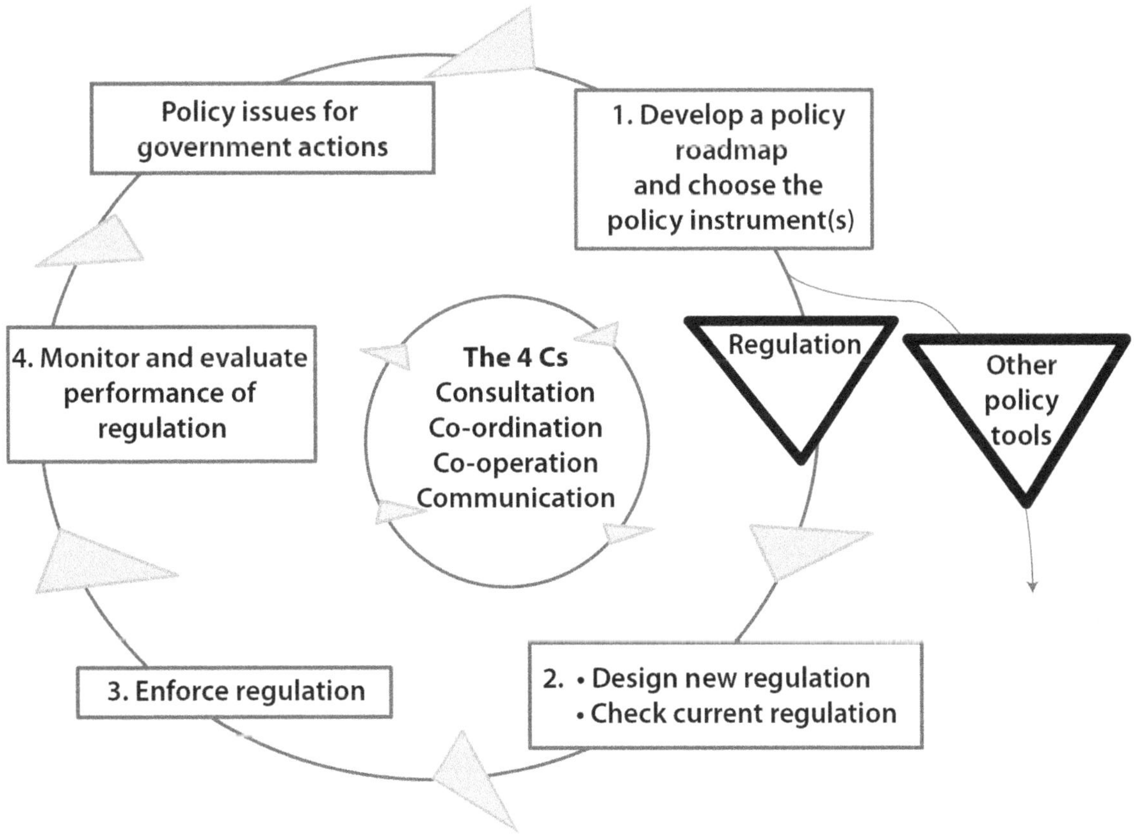

Source: (OECD, 2011[7]), *Regulatory Policy and Governance: Supporting Economic Growth and Serving the Public Interest*, OECD Publishing, Paris, http://dx.doi.org/10.1787/9789264116573-en.

The regulatory governance cycle has four main stages: development of public policy and choice of instruments; design of new regulation (or review of the existing one); implementation of regulation; and monitoring and evaluation of its effects (OECD, 2011[7]). The prelude to this analysis, however, is the identification of the policy problem and that it requires government intervention.

RIA is an element that allows measuring the relevance of the regulations versus the public policy objectives. Consequently, RIA should be conducted between steps 1 and 3: the definition of the public policy problem and the application and enforcement of the regulation. RIA takes part in the identification of the problem through an early consultation with the interested or possible affected parties, in order to prepare a description of the problem, make adjustments, or elaborate on the problem identified by public officials. With this information, it is possible to prepare a public policy proposal and choose the intervention instruments (step 1).

Afterwards, the RIA helps to choose the best option for the government to step in, either with regulatory or other type of mechanisms; to this end, it uses the cost-benefit analysis, among other cost-analysis tools. The final design of the regulation is part of the RIA process, which includes an additional consultation process that should be more open and aimed to adjust the regulatory instruments used (step 2). This consultation process is very important so that regulations are as adequate as possible, because it allows identifying omissions, biases, unidentified effects, and so forth. Box 1.3 shows an example of how the consultation process is carried out in one of the OECD countries.

Box 1.3. Public consultations in Canada

In Canada, the adequacy of consultations conducted by the ministries with the representatives involved—prior to seeking the Cabinet's weighing of a regulatory proposal, along with the result of the consultations, such as the support from the interested parties—plays an important role to determine if the Cabinet will approve the pre-publication of the proposal to obtain feedback from the general public.

In 2009, the government of Canada issued a Guide for an Effective Regulatory Consultation, the guidelines offer information on the components of effective regulatory consultations, along with checklists about:

- Ongoing, constructive, and professional relationship with stakeholders
- Consultation plan
  - Statement of purpose and objectives
  - Analysis of the public environment
  - Development of realistic timelines
  - Internal and interdepartmental co-ordination
  - Selection of consultation tools
  - Selection of participants
  - Effective budgeting
  - Ongoing evaluation, end-of-process evaluation, and documentation
  - Feedback/follow-up
- At the moment of conducting the consultations
  - Communicating neutral, relevant, and timely information
  - Ensuring that officials in charge of the consultation have the necessary skills

Source: (Government of Canada, 2007[8]), "Guidelines for Effective Regulatory Consultations", www.tbs-sct.gc.ca/rtrap-parfa/erc-cer/erc-cer01-eng.asp (accessed July 2018).

The regulatory governance cycle continues with the implementation of regulations and its monitoring and evaluation. This stage closes the loop, by identifying new problems and public policy objectives that should lead to adjustments in the instruments created, either at design or implementation level.

It should be noted that the implementation of the regulatory governance cycle should be carried out considering four principles of efficiency and modern governance: consultation, co-ordination, co-operation, and communication. These principles should align the participation of civil society with the different government entities and national and international organisations.

Note

[1] In this survey, regulations, rules and regulation are synonymous, and they refer to the legal instruments issued by a government authority that establish obligations, restrictions, or rights for companies and citizens in a specific jurisdiction.

References

Government of Canada (2007), *Guidelines for Effective Regulatory Consultations - Canada.ca*, https://www.canada.ca/en/treasury-board-secretariat/services/federal-regulatory-management/guidelines-tools/effective-regulatory-consultations.html (accessed on 26 April 2018). [8]

OECD (2015), *OECD Regulatory Policy Outlook 2015*, OECD Publishing, Paris, https://dx.doi.org/10.1787/9789264238770-en. [3]

OECD (2015), *Regulatory Policy in Perspective: A Reader's Companion to the OECD Regulatory Policy Outlook 2015*, OECD Publishing, Paris, https://dx.doi.org/10.1787/9789264241800-en. [4]

OECD (2014), *Regulatory Policy in Mexico: Towards a Whole-of-Government Perspective to Regulatory Improvement*, OECD Reviews of Regulatory Reform, OECD Publishing, Paris, https://dx.doi.org/10.1787/9789264203389-en. [2]

OECD (2012), *Recommendation of the Council on Regulatory Policy and Governance*, OECD Publishing, Paris, https://dx.doi.org/10.1787/9789264209022-en. [1]

OECD (2011), *Regulatory Policy and Governance: Supporting Economic Growth and Serving the Public Interest*, OECD Publishing, Paris, https://dx.doi.org/10.1787/9789264116573-en. [7]

OECD (2008), *Introductory Handbook for Undertaking Regulatory Impact Analysis (RIA)*, OECD, https://www.oecd.org/gov/regulatory-policy/44789472.pdf (accessed on 3 August 2017). [5]

Querbach, T. and C. Arndt (2017), "Regulatory policy in Latin America: An analysis of the state of play", *OECD Regulatory Policy Working Papers*, No. 7, OECD Publishing, Paris, https://dx.doi.org/10.1787/2cb29d8c-en. [6]

Chapter 2. Methodology to analyse regulatory impact assessment in Peru

This chapter describes the methodology employed to elaborate this document, which consists of the following stages: 1) Selection of the ministries covered in the survey and the regulation that will be considered as the basis for the design of the current process for the issuance of regulation; 2) Fact-finding missions to collect information; 3) Desk work that includes the review of the legal framework in place and the information obtained; f) Comparative analysis between the current process for the issuance of regulation and the best international practices to define the ideal process to issue regulation in Peru.

The purpose of this survey is to contribute to the establishment of an efficient and effective process for the issuance of regulation in the central government of Peru, taking advantage of the regulatory impact assessment as an analytical tool to control the quality of regulations that are issued through the Executive Branch. International practices will be taken into account for the design of the ideal process, which will be adapted to the conditions and needs of the Peruvian government. The objective is to make this process effective and efficient when it comes to address the different problems that require government intervention.

The methodology used to conduct this document consists of the following phases described in this chapter: the first, selection of the ministries covered in this report, which will integrate the pilot programme for the adoption of RIA within the central government. It also describes the process of choosing the regulations that served as a reference to the ministries to describe the current process for the issuance of regulation. The second phase consists of two fact-finding missions to gather first-hand information from the public officials directly involved in the rule-making process. The third, which comprises desk work and examination of the current legal framework applicable to the rule-making process, as well as the analysis of all the information gathered by the fact-finding missions, to be able to determine the current process followed by the central government for the issuance of regulation. Finally, a comparative analysis between the current process for the issuance of regulations and the best international practices, to create the ideal process that is suggested for the issuance of regulations originating in the Executive Branch.

Selection of ministries and regulations

At the beginning of the preparation of this report, it was resolved, in the first place, which ministries would be included in the pilot program for the implementation of RIA. To this end, five ministries that often issue regulations or whose regulation affects a large number of economic units were selected.[1] These ministries are shown in Table 2.1.

Table 2.1. Selected ministries

Ministry of Economy and Finance (MEF)
Ministry of Environment (MINAM)
Ministry of Transport and Communications (MTC)
Ministry of Production (PRODUCE)
Ministry of Housing, Construction and Sanitation (VIVIENDA)

Once the ministries were determined, a search was made in the *Official Gazette El Peruano*[2] of the regulations issued by those ministries, to select the one that would be the basis to describe the process for the issuance of regulations currently carried out in Peru. As the survey focuses on the regulation originating in the Executive Branch, the following characteristics of the regulation were considered to select the instruments:

- Instruments arising from the Executive Branch;
- Of general nature, and
- With probable impact on businesses or citizens (may also have an impact on the public and social spheres).

The Political Constitution of Peru, Articles 107 and 118, paragraph 8, establishes the power of the President to issue regulation (laws and bylaws, and in the latter, he/she is empowered to issue decrees and resolutions).

Given what was mentioned above, and in accordance with the concepts stated in the *Guide on Legislative Technique for the Development of Regulatory Proposals from the Entities of the Executive Branch*, the types of regulation considered are described in Table 2.2.

Table 2.2. Types of regulation to consider

Type of regulation	Description
Bill or draft	Formal document containing the draft of a law that, according to the Political Constitution of Peru, the President has the power to submit before the Congress of the Republic for its study, discussion and, if appropriate, approval.
Legislative decrees	Law-level regulation arising from the Executive Branch by virtue of an explicit authorisation from the Congress of the Republic by means of authoritative law. These rules have a material and temporary limit.
Supreme decrees	General norms that regulate law-level rules or regulate sectoral functional or multisectoral functional activity at national level, and through which the President exercises the power to regulate the laws, without transgressing or denaturing them. These may or may not require the approving vote from the Council of Ministers, as provided for by the law, they also should be signed by the President of the Republic and endorsed by one or several of the relevant ministers.
Ministerial resolutions	Rules that allow for the development, implementation, and oversight of national and sectoral policies under the responsibility of a state minister. They are approved by the corresponding state minister.
Vice-ministerial resolutions	Norms that regulate specific aspects within a certain sector.

For the purposes of this document, directorate resolutions were not taken into account, since they are norms regulating the exercise of duties in entities from a specific sector, according to their organisation and obligations.

A two-year consultation period, from 2 June 2014 to 30 June 2016, was established to select the regulation of each ministry. The idea was to have a timeframe long enough to ensure the inclusion of current and relevant regulation; but that, in turn, such period did not compromise the effectiveness of the regulation, that is, that it became updated.

When the search of regulation was made in *El Peruano* website, the following search parameters were used, as stated therein:

- What do you want to look for?
- What do you want to exclude from the results?
- Type of publication
- Publication date (from-to)
- Entity group
- Entity

Considering these parameters, the following information was obtained:

- **Ministry of Economy and Finance:** 1 580 instruments, including supreme decrees, supreme, ministerial, vice-ministerial, directorate, and chief resolutions.
- **Ministry of Environment:** 293 instruments, including supreme decrees, ministerial and supreme resolutions.

- **Ministry of Transport and Communications:** 3 013 instruments, including supreme decrees, ministerial, vice-ministerial, and directorate resolutions.
- **Ministry of Production:** 949 instruments, including supreme decrees, executive, ministerial, and directorate resolutions.
- **Ministry of Housing, Construction and Sanitation:** 463 instruments, including supreme decrees, ministerial, supreme, and vice-ministerial resolutions.

It was observed, in the list of regulations obtained, that a large number of them are directly related to approvals for officials to leave the country and attend international commitments, others are of a particular and not general nature; some address internal norms or regulate internal conditions in the public administration—internal management procedures, appointments and resignations of officials, creation of working groups, authorisations of events, among other regulatory instruments. In particular, apart from the previous ones, in the case of the MEF, there is also a large number of supreme decrees related to the transfer of line items in the public budget; in the MINAM, there is a large number of ministerial resolutions aimed to recognise private preservation areas; in the MTC, there is a large number of authorisations to render broadcasting services; in PRODUCE, rules regarding the cancellation of extractive activities of certain marine resources and regulation about the organisation and operation of public entities; and, lastly, in VIVIENDA, various regulations related to the water service of the provinces are published, as well as authorisations of different programs and appointments of officials before diverse entities.

All the regulations mentioned above were not taken into account for the purposes of this study. Annex 2.A lists the regulation selected for each of the ministries.

Afterwards, the information was sent to the ministries for them to choose three instruments, which served as the basis to describe the current process for the issuance of regulations. A questionnaire was also prepared, which was sent to the five ministries to gather information on the practices that they follow for the issuance of regulations and identify those that – according to international practices – are not carried out or are done, but not in a standardised way. Once the questionnaires were completed, the information gathered was analysed along with the regulatory framework in place, in order to identify both in practice and in theory, the activities carried out in the five ministries; and be able to establish a harmonised process for the issuance of regulations and define the opportunity areas for the adoption of an ideal process.

Fact-finding missions

Two fact-finding missions were carried out, as outlined in Table 2.3:

Table 2.3. Fact-finding missions to implement RIA in Peru

Mission	Date	Description
First	21-24 November 2016	Objective: to hold meetings with the selected ministries to collect information about the rule-making process and to carry out the corresponding mapping by ministry, as well as a general mapping of the elements from the regulatory process in Peru.
Second	3-4 April 2017	Objective: to submit and discuss the preliminary results, which included presenting the identified mappings of the public policy processes of the regulation, as well as the initial diagnosis of the elements from the RIA system and get feedback from the ministries.

The goal of the first fact-finding mission was to gather first-hand information from the ministries covered in this survey about the procedure and practices carried out during the process to issue regulations. To this end, several meetings were held both with the ministries and with other entities participating in this process, such as the MINJUSDH and the PCM.

In the second fact-finding mission, the objective was to present the general process followed for the issuance of regulation. The purpose was to get feedback from the ministries and the various entities involved in this process; and to be able to define a general process, as well as the ideal one and the necessary steps to achieve it.

Moreover, as part of the activities of these missions, on 14-15 December 2016, a training workshop on regulatory impact and consultation was delivered, in which several ministries participated.

Analysis of the current process and definition of the ideal process

First, desk work of the applicable legal framework was made in order to define the current process followed by Peru for the issuance of regulations. For this purpose, the following regulatory instruments were mainly considered (see Chapter 4):

- Organic Law of the Executive Branch (N° 29158)
- Law on the General Administrative Procedure (N° 27444)
- Framework Law for Legislative Production and Systematization (N° 26889)
- Bylaw of the Framework Law for Legislative Production and Systematization (N° 008-2006-JUS)
- Bylaw that lays down rules on advertising, publication of regulatory proposals, and dissemination of general legal rules (N° 001-2009-JUS)
- Guide on Legislative Technique for the Development of Regulatory Proposals from the Entities of the Executive Branch (N° 007-2016-JUS/DGDOJ)
- Specific rules applicable to the ministries regarding their powers and sphere of competence for the issuance of regulations.

Parallel to the analysis of the regulatory framework, the information provided by the ministries through the questionnaires and the data collected in the interviews carried out during the first fact-finding mission was also analysed. Considering these sources of information, a first general process was identified, which highlighted the general practices performed in all the ministries, as well as the individual ones that, as appropriate, are carried out in each of them. In this case, it was noted that the MINAM is the ministry with the most complete regulatory practices; unlike the other ministries, it formally carries out – among other practices – an early consultation with stakeholders that, in most cases, is useful to define the problem and its scale and, consequently, the best alternative to solve it.

In the second fact-finding mission, the identified process was presented to the participating ministries, both for its validation and for their comments; and the final general process that is currently carried out in Peru for the issuance of regulations was defined (see Chapter 5).

Afterwards, a comparative analysis was made between the current regulatory issuance process in Peru and the RIA building blocks to identify the steps that are not considered by the Peruvian government (see Chapter 6). This analysis was the basis for the recommendations aimed at the modification the process followed by Peru and for the systematic incorporation of the RIA as a tool to ensure the quality of the regulations and adopting best international practices (see Chapters 7 and 8).

Once this analysis was concluded, the ideal process for the issuance of regulations in Peru was prepared; which was presented, along with the recommendations, in a meeting held with the MEF during the month of June 2017.

Notes

[1] The definition employed in this survey for economic units is: entities producing goods and services, either establishments, households or individuals.

[2] http://diariooficial.elperuano.pe/.

Reference

OECD (2016), *Regulatory Policy in Peru: Assembling the Framework for Regulatory Quality*, OECD Publishing, Paris, http://dx.doi.org/10.1787/9789264260054-en.

Annex 2.A. Selection of legal instruments to evaluate the process of issuing regulations in Peru

Economy and finance

- Supreme Decree N° 164-2016-EF

Inclusion of operations in Appendix V of the Unique Ordered Text of the Law on General Sales Tax and Selective Excise Tax (*Inclusión de operaciones en el Apéndice V del Texto Único Ordenado de la Ley del Impuesto General a las Ventas e Impuesto Selectivo al Consumo*)

- Supreme Decree N° 151-2016-EF (*Decreto Supremo* N° 151-2016-EF)

They modify the Supreme Decree N° 051-2008-EF (*Decreto Supremo* N° 051-2008-EF) that regulates the reimbursement of undue payments or in excess of tax debts whose administration is in charge of the SUNAT by means of Payment Orders of the Financial System

- Supreme Decree N° 100 2016-EF (*Decreto Supremo* N° 100-2016-EF)

They modify the Bylaw of Law N° 29623 (*Reglamento de la Ley* N° 2962) that promotes financing through commercial invoices, approved by Supreme Decree N° 208-2015-EF (*Decreto Supremo* N° 208-2015-EF)

- Supreme Decree N° 059-2016-EF (*Decreto Supremo* N° 059-2016-EF)

They modify Articles 2, 19, 27, 28 and 29 from the Bylaw of Legislative Decree N° 1126 (*Reglamento del Decreto Legislativo* N° 1126), that establishes control measures for chemical inputs and controlled products, machinery and equipment used for the production of illicit drugs, approved by Supreme Decree N° 044-2013-EF (*Decreto Supremo* N° 044-2013-EF) and amendments thereof.

- Supreme Decree N° 006-2016-EF (*Decreto Supremo* N° 006-2016-EF)

Approval of regulatory standards from Law N° 30220, University Law (*Ley Universitaria*), regarding the tax credit for reinvestment.

- Supreme Decree N° 119-2015-EF (*Decreto Supremo* N° 119-2015-E)

They modify the Supreme Decree N° 073-2014-EF (*Decreto Supremo* N° 073-2014-EF) that issues regulatory standards for the application of the First Final Supplementary Provision from the Legislative Decree N° 1103[1] (*Primera Disposición Complementaria Final del Derecho Legislativo* N° 1103).

Environment

- Ministerial Resolution N° 090-2016-MINAM (*Resolución Ministerial* N° 090-2016-MINAM)

Approval of Guidelines for the Integrated Management of Climate Change and the Climate Management Initiative (*Lineamientos para la Gestión Integrada del Cambio Climático y la Iniciativa Gestión Clima*)

- Ministerial Resolution N° 066-2016-MINAM (*Resolución Ministerial* N° 066-2016-MINAM)

Approval of the "General Guide for the Environmental Compensation Plan" (Guía General para el Plan de Compensación Ambiental)

- Ministerial Resolution N° 023-2015-MINAM (*Resolución Ministerial* N° 023-2015-MINAM)

Approval of "Summary of Guides to be applied in the Control and Surveillance Procedures for the detection of Living Modified Organisms – LMO" (*Compendio de Guías a ser aplicadas en los Procedimientos de Control y Vigilancia para la detección de Organismos Vivos Modificados—OVM*)

- Ministerial Resolution N° 398-2014-MINAM (*Resolución Ministerial* N° 398-2014-MINAM)

Approval of Guidelines for Environmental Compensation in the frame of the National System for the Environmental Impact Assessment – SEIA (*Lineamientos para la Compensación Ambiental en el marco del Sistema Nacional de Evaluación de Impacto Ambiental*—SEIA)

- Supreme Decree N° 015-2015-MINAM (*Decreto Supremo* N° 013-2015-MINAM)

They modify the National Environmental Quality Standards for Water and establish supplementary provisions for its application (*Estándares Nacionales de Calidad Ambiental para Agua y establecen disposiciones complementarias para su aplicación*)

- Supreme Decree N° 013-2015-MINAM (Decreto Supremo N° 013-2015-MINAM)

They issue rules for the submission and assessment of the Report on the Identification of Polluted Sites (*Informe de Identificación de Sitios Contaminados*).

- Supreme Decree N° 010-2014-MINAM (*Decreto Supremo* N° 010-2014-MINAM)

Supreme Decree that modifies Articles 3, 33, 34 and 35 and integrates two annexes in the Bylaw of Law N° 29811, approved by Supreme Decree N° 008-2012-MINAM (*Decreto Supremo* N° 008-2012-MINAM) on the control of entry into national territory of living modified organisms.

Transport

- Supreme Decree N° 009-2016-MTC (*Decreto Supremo* N° 009-2016-MTC)

Supreme Decree that modifies the National Regulations of Vehicular Technical Inspections and the Unique Ordered Text of the National Traffic Regulations (*Reglamento Nacional de Inspecciones Técnicas Vehiculares y el Texto Único Ordenado del Reglamento Nacional de Tránsito*)

- Supreme Decree N° 008-2016-MTC (*Decreto Supremo* N° 008-2016-MTC)

Supreme Decree that modifies the Bylaw of the Radio and Television Law (*Reglamento de la Ley de Radio y Televisión*), approved by Supreme Decree N° 005-2005-MTC (*Decreto Supremo* N° 005-2005-MTC)

- Supreme Decree N° 003-2016-MTC (*Decreto Supremo* N° 003-2016-MTC)

Supreme Decree that modifies the Supreme Decree N° 023-2014-MTC (*Decreto Supremo* N° 023-2014-MTC) and provides for the use of a Biometric Mechanism to validate the identity of subscribers of Prepaid Mobile Public Services

- Supreme Decree N° 006-2016-MTC (*Decreto Supremo* N° 006-2016-MTC)

Approval of modifications to the Unique Ordered Text of the National Transit Regulations, Transit Code and the National Bylaw on Transport Administration (*Texto Único Ordenado del Reglamento Nacional de Tránsito – Código de Tránsito y al Reglamento Nacional de Administración de Transporte*).

- Supreme Decree N° 001-2016-MTC (*Decreto Supremo* N° 001-2016-MTC)

Supreme Decree that modifies the Unique Ordered Text of the General Regulations of Telecommunications Law (*Texto Único Ordenado del Reglamento General de la Ley de Telecomunicaciones)*

- Supreme Decree N° 013-2015-MTC (*Decreto Supremo* N° 013-2015-MTC)

Supreme Decree that modifies the First Transitory Supplementary Provision of Supreme Decree N° 025-2014-MTC and lays down other provisions (*Primera Disposición Complementaria Transitoria del Decreto Supremo* N° 025-2014-MTC *y establece otras disposiciones*).

- Ministerial Resolution N° 303-2016 MTC/01.02 (*Resolución Ministerial* N° 303-2016 MTC/01.02)

Draft Supreme Decree approving modifications to the Unique Ordered Text of the National Transit Regulations – Transit Code, approved by Supreme Decree N° 016-2009-MTC (*Texto Único Ordenado del Reglamento Nacional de Tránsito – Código de Tránsito, aprobado por Decreto Supremo* N° 016-2009-MTC)

Produce

- Supreme Decree N° 009-2016-PRODUCE (*Decreto Supremo* N° 009-2016-PRODUCE)

They establish measures to strengthen the fishing industry when processing the tuna resource

- Supreme Decree N° 006-2016-PRODUCE (*Decreto Supremo* N° 006-2016-PRODUCE

They establish general provisions to strengthen small-scale fishing in the production chain

- Supreme Decree N° 003-2016-PRODUCE (*Decreto Supremo* N° 003-2016-PRODUCE)

Approval of the Bylaw of the General Law on Aquaculture, approved by Legislative Decree N° 1195 (*Reglamento de la Ley General de Acuicultura, aprobada por Decreto Legislativo* N° 1195)

- Supreme Decree N° 021-2015-PRODUCE (*Decreto Supremo* N° 021-2015-PRODUCE)

Approval of the Bylaw of the National Registry of Associations of Micro and Small-size Enterprises – RENAMYPE (*Reglamento del Registro Nacional de Asociaciones de la Micro y Pequeña Empresa – RENAMYPE)*

- Ministerial Resolution N° 196-2016-PRODUCE (*Resolución Ministerial* N° 196-2016-PRODUCE)

Ministerial Resolution approving General Guidelines of National Policy for the Competitiveness of Provisions Markets (*Lineamientos Generales de la Política Nacional para la Competitividad de Mercados de Abastos*)

Vivienda

- Supreme Decree N° 017-2015-VIVIENDA (*Decreto Supremo* N° 017-2015-VIVIENDA)

Supreme Decree approving the Bylaw of Legislative Decree N° 1177, Legislative Decree that establishes the Promotion Scheme of Leasing for Housing (*Reglamento del Decreto Legislativo* N° 1177, *Decreto Legislativo que establece el Régimen de Promoción al Arrendamiento para Vivienda*)

- Supreme Decree N° 002-2016-VIVIENDA (*Decreto Supremo* N° 002-2016-VIVIENDA)

Supreme Decree approving the Bylaw of Chapter I of Title IV of Law N° 30327, Law on Promotion of Investments for Economic Growth and Sustainable Development (*Decreto Supremo que aprueba el Reglamento del Capítulo* I *del Título* IV *de la Ley* N° 30327, *Ley de Promoción a las Inversiones para el Crecimiento Económico y el Desarrollo Sostenible*)

- Supreme Decree N° 006-2016-VIVIENDA (*Decreto Supremo* N° 006-2016-VIVIENDA)

Supreme Decree approving Bylaw of Law N° 29203, Law that creates the Information Center of Real Estate Developers and/or Construction Companies of Real State Units (*Reglamento de la Ley* N° 2920, *Ley que crea la Central de Información de Promotores Inmobiliarios y/o Empresas Constructoras de Unidades Inmobiliarias*)

- Ministerial Resolution N° 330-2015-VIVIENDA (*Resolución Ministerial* N° 330-2015-VIVIENDA)

They modify the operating bylaws approved through Ministerial Resolutions N° 102 and 209-2012-VIVIENDA, to adapt them to provisions contained in the Law that creates the Family Housing Bonus (BFH)

- Ministerial Resolution N° 326-2015-VIVIENDA (*Resolución Ministerial* N° 326-2015-VIVIENDA)

Approval of forms regarding procedures of licenses for urban fit out and edification licenses.

Others

Irrespective of the above legal instruments, the legislative decrees issued during the same period were also consulted, finding 74 instruments, 19 of which relate to security issues and 17 are errata; therefore, from the remaining ones the following are suggested to be considered:

- Legislative Decree N° 1205 (*Decreto Legislativo* N° 1205)

Legislative Decree modifying Legislative Decree N° 1034, that approves the Law on Suppression of Anticompetitive Behaviors (*Decreto Legislativo que modifica el Decreto Legislativo* N° 1034, *que aprueba la Ley de Represión de Conductas Anticompetitivas*)

- Legislative Decree N° 1209 (*Decreto Legislativo* N° 1209)

Legislative Decree establishing the procedure to be followed for the registration (original entry) of privately owned property in the Land Registry (*Decreto Legislativo que Establece el Procedimineto a seguir para la Inmatriculación de Predios de Propiedad Privada de Particulares en el Registro de Predios*)

- Legislative Decree N° 1212 (*Decreto Legislativo* N° 1212)

Legislative Decree strengthening the powers on the elimination of bureaucratic barriers for the promotion of competitiveness (Decreto Legislativo que Refuerza las Facultades sobre Eliminación de Barreras Burocráticas para el Fomento de la Competitividad)

- Legislative Decree N° 1232 (*Decreto Legislativo* N° 1232)

Legislative Decree that modifies various articles and Transitory and Final Supplementary Provisions of Legislative Decree N° 1049, Legislative Decree of Notaries (*Decreto Legislativo que Modifica Diversos Artículos y Disposiciones Complementarisa Transitorias y Finales del Derecho Legislativo* N° 1049, *Decreto Legislativo del Notariado).*

Note

[1] This decree was published on 26 May 2015, but it was considered relevant to include it to have a greater variety of regulation covered by the review by the Ministry of Economy and Finance.

Chapter 3. Regulatory impact assessment systems in OECD countries

This chapter addresses the regulatory practices of Australia, Canada, Mexico, and the European Union. In the case of countries such as Australia and Canada, the law does not require preparing a Regulatory Impact Assessment, but it is laid down in specific guidelines that oblige public entities to carry it out. In addition, it explains the criteria employed to define when it has to be performed and its level of analysis. Finally, it outlines the steps that are followed in different countries to prepare the RIA, as well as the cases in which the public consultation is used and how it is conducted.

RIA Obligation and entity in charge

The quality of a country's regulatory policy is an issue that affects both citizens and business and is related to the design, assessment, and compliance with legislation. The obligation of conducting a Regulatory Impact Assessment varies by country and region and is primarily ruled by the law of each place, either Anglo Saxon (common law) or Roman law. Irrespective of the law governing, the OECD Recommendations (OECD, 2012[1]) refer to the need of committing at the highest political level to the development of quality public policies. For this reason, assessing the regulation is an issue that is incumbent upon the entire government and it usually involves the creation of an oversight body or the appointment of an official in charge of that task.

This chapter documents the experience of the RIA system in Australia, Canada, Mexico, and the European Union. As indicated in Table 3.1, the countries considered in this section have provisions that establish the obligation of assessing regulations before issued. Furthermore, most of them have a specialised entity in charge of ensuring compliance with the best practices of regulatory policy.

Table 3.1. RIA obligation, entity in charge, and implementation guidelines

Country/region	Obligation to apply the RIA	Entity in charge of the RIA
Australia	A RIA is mandatory for all regulations submitted before the Cabinet, even if there are no obvious regulatory impacts.	The Office of Best Practice Regulation (OBPR) is a body that works exclusively as a gatekeeper and advisor for the preparation of assessments.
Canada	It is mandatory to submit a RIA based on the Cabinet Directive for rulemaking, from which it arises the Guide to Prepare Laws and Regulations.	There is no body in charge of the regulatory policy, it is a responsibility shared by the Prime Minister and the ministry, the Leader of Government in the House of Commons, the Cabinet and its members, and the Minister of Justice
Mexico	It is mandatory for the creation or modification of primary and subordinate regulations from the Executive Branch, with the exception of the Ministries of National Defense and of Navy.	The public governing body in charge is the Federal Commission for Regulatory Improvement, an administrative body sectored to the Ministry of Economy.
European Union	The RIA is mandatory for initiatives (legislative and non-legislative) with important economic, environmental or social effects.	The Impact Assessment Board (IAB), it is the technical arm of the European Commission that analyses the RIA process.

Source: Prepared by the OECD, based on: (Government of Australia, 2016[2]), "User Guide to the Australian Government Guide to Regulation", https://www.pmc.gov.au/resource-centre/regulation/user-guide-australian-government-guide-regulation; (Government of Canada, 2014[3]), "Guide to the Federal Regulatory Development Process" in "Guidelines and Tools", https://www.canada.ca/en/treasury-board-secretariat/services/federal-regulatory-management/guidelines-tools/guide-federal-regulatory-development-process.html#t1; (CONAMER, 2017[4]), Government portal, www.conamer.gob.mx (accessed 28 June 2017); (European Commission, 2009[5]), "Impact Assessment Guidelines", http://ec.europa.eu/smart-regulation/impact/commission_guidelines/docs/iag_2009_en.pdf.

The existence of a manual or guide to prepare the regulatory impact assessment is a key point OECD countries converge. According to (OECD, 2015[6]), 34 of the OECD countries have some type of document stating the requirements and guidelines that must be observed when issuing regulation. In the case studies covered in this section, all the countries or regions have, at least, a manual specifying the criteria for the conduction of the RIA. The following are the most important documents for each country:

- **Australia:** The Australian Government Guide to Regulation
- **Canada:** Guide for the editor of the Regulatory Impact Assessment Statements (RIA-S)
- **Mexico:** Manual for the Development of the Regulatory Impact Expression (MIR, by its initials in Spanish)
- **European Union:** Impact Assessment Guidelines of the European Commission

These documents can be the basis to develop a RIA manual that meets the highest international standards.

Moreover, the entity in charge of supervising the regulatory impact assessment tends to be external to the agency issuing the regulation, and close to the central government. This agency must ensure the quality of the regulatory policy, identify the opportunity areas where regulation can be more efficient, as well as deliver training and clear up the doubts of the parties involved (OECD, 2012[1]).

Evaluation criteria to determine the RIA and its classification

As the thorough analysis of all the regulations issued may be an expensive and inefficient exercise, countries have established criteria to determine which proposals to assess and the scope of such assessment. Some countries, such as Australia and from the European Union, have a proportionality analysis, which allows them to use more efficiently the available resources by focusing on assessing only the regulation with a high impact on citizens or business, or proposals that may be controversial.

Australia employs three types of RIA based on the characteristics of the regulatory proposal (Table 3.2). As mentioned in the next section, the requirements that must be met for each of the three types are different, those related to the long RIA are the most difficult and strict ones.

Table 3.2. RIA Categories in Australia

Short	Standard	Long
Characteristics of the regulatory proposal		
1. The topic of public policy is simple, well defined or the alternatives are limited. 2. The policy addresses issues of national security, public safety, natural disasters or a high-pressure event. 3. The regulatory impact of the policy is of low priority. 4. Recently, a RIA was completed and only minor modifications have been made to the public policy options under consideration. 5. The proposal is not regulatory, or is small.	1. The policy proposal has an impact on the economy that is measurable, but contained. 2. The proposed changes affect a number relatively small of companies, civil organisations, and individuals. 3. The administrative and compliance costs are measurable, but not high. 4. Strong opposition between the relevant actors or the public is unlikely. 5. The subject matter is not controversial and it is unlikely that it calls the attention of the media.	1. The policy proposal has considerable or broad effects on the economy. 2. The proposed changes affect a large number of companies, civil organisations, or individuals. 3. Administrative or compliance costs are high. 4. There may be a firm opposition from the relevant actors or the public. 5. The subject matter is sensitive, controversial, or it may call the attention of the media.

Source: Prepared by the OECD, based on (Government of Australia, 2016[2]), "User Guide to the Australian Government Guide to Regulation", https://www.pmc.gov.au/resource-centre/regulation/user-guide-australian-government-guide-regulation (accessed 28 June 2017).

In the case of Canada, the process to determine the type of Regulatory Impact Assessment (RIA) to be carried out depends primarily on the cost of the regulation. Based on the answers to items 2 and 3 of the triage statement (Figure 3.1), it is decided whether a low-impact or medium-high impact RIA is prepared. The office in charge of regulatory matters within the Treasury Board must approve the triage statement to prepare the assessment.

Figure 3.1. Triage statement in Canada

1. Benefits of the proposal
2. Costs to the government, business (industry), consumers and Canadians
3. Other costs and distributional issues
4. Public interest, stakeholder support or potential controversy
5. Regulatory co-ordination and co-operation
6. International agreements, obligations and standards
7. Legal risk, policy or government priorities or miscellaneous amendment regulations (MARs)
8. "One-for-One" rule and small business lens

Source: Prepared by the OECD with information from (Government of Canada, 2014[7]), "Triage Statement Form" in "Guidelines and Tools", https://www.canada.ca/en/treasury-board-secretariat/services/federal-regulatory-management/guidelines-tools/triage-statement-form.html (accessed 28 June 2017).

In Mexico, all regulations must go through an assessment process whenever the compliance costs are greater than zero. If they are equal to zero, it is not necessary to submit a RIA. The *Regulatory Impact Calculator* determines the potential impact of a regulatory proposal. This is a software tool consisting of ten questions to determine the type of RIA to be conducted. Furthermore, the Calculator indicates if it is necessary that the National Commission for Regulatory Improvement (CONAMER)[1] prepares a competition analysis, and/or a risk analysis. Table 3.3 shows the four types of RIA for regulatory proposals in Mexico.

Table 3.3. Types of RIA in Mexico

Moderate impact	High impact	Periodic updating	Emergency
The result of the potential impact from the Regulatory Impact Calculator is moderate	The result of the potential impact from the Regulatory Impact Calculator is high or the COFEMER so requires	For draft regulations that modify provisions on a regular basis and do not imply additional costs	If the proposal is classified as emergency regulation

Source: Prepared by the OECD, based on (CONAMER, 2017[4]), Government portal, www.cofemer.gob.mx (accessed 28 June 2017).

In the European Union, RIA must be carried out when there are important economic, environmental or social impacts of the regulation, and they are analysed on a case-by-case basis. There are initiatives that do not require any RIA at all, for example, administrative decisions, reports and statements from the European Union, as well as budgetary procedures and decisions related to the administration of programs. Should a RIA must be prepared, the proportionality criteria help determining its level and thoroughness. Some of the factors that can influence such thoroughness are the political importance of the initiative, at what stage is the policy, the scale and complexity of the problem under analysis, the importance of the expected impacts, the complexity of the necessary requirements to observe the regulation, and the risk of unforeseen negative consequences.

RIA analysis process

OECD member countries increasingly use the RIA process when they issue legislation, but the way it is incorporated into the regulatory policy cycle varies upon the country. This section highlights best practices followed by leading countries in terms of regulatory impact.

As mentioned above, Australia has three types of RIA: short, standard and long. Table 3.4 shows the requirements for each type. The standard and long RIA are both similar and require the regulator to answer seven basic questions (see Box 3.1). The long type RIA however includes a formal analysis of the costs and benefits of the regulatory proposal.

Table 3.4. Requirements for the RIA in Australia

Requirements for each type of RIA		
Short	Standard	Long
1. Summary both of the proposed policy and the alternatives considered 2. An overview of the possible impacts 3. An outline of regulatory costs and cost offsets	1. Answer the seven questions from the RIA 2. Analysis of genuine and practical alternatives 3. Analysis of the potential regulatory impacts 4. Evidence of an appropriate public consultation 5. A detailed presentation of regulatory costings and offsets	1. Answer the seven questions from the RIA 2. Analysis of genuine and practical alternatives 3. Analysis of the potential regulatory impacts 4. Evidence of an adequate public consultation 5. A formal costs-benefit analysis 6. A detailed presentation of regulatory costings and offsets

Source: Prepared by the OECD, based on (Government of Australia, 2016[2]), "User Guide to the Australian Government Guide to Regulation", https://www.pmc.gov.au/resource-centre/regulation/user-guide-australian-government-guide-regulation (accessed 28 June 2017).

Table 3.5. Regulatory impact assessments in Canada

Low impact	Medium-high impact
1. Brief description of the problem	1. Executive summary
2. Information about the context (if applicable)	2. Information about the context (if applicable)
3. Objectives	3. Description of the problem
4. Description of the proposed regulation	4. Alternatives considered (including, not regulating)
5. Compliance with the "one-for-one" rule	5. Costs and benefits
6. Small business lens (if applicable)	6. Compliance with the "one-for-one" rule
7. Public consultation (if applicable)	7. Small business lens
8. Rationale for the proposed regulation	8. Public consultation
9. Implementation, enforcement and oversight (if applicable)	9. Regulatory co-operation
	10. Rationale for the proposed regulation
	11. Implementation, enforcement and monitoring
	12. Measurement of the accomplishment of goals and assessment (if applicable)

Notes: The "one-for-one" rule controls the administrative burden on business by requiring that all administrative burdens imposed by new regulation be accompanied by an equivalent reduction of administrative burdens.
Source: (Government of Canada, 2014[3]), "Guide to the Federal Regulatory Development Process" in "Guidelines and Tools", https://www.canada.ca/en/treasury-board-secretariat/services/federal-regulatory-management/guidelines-tools/guide-federal-regulatory-development-process.html#t1 (accessed 28 June 2017); (Government of Canada, 2014[8]), "Regulatory Impact Analysis Statement: Low-Impact Template", https://www.canada.ca/en/treasury-board-secretariat/services/federal-regulatory-management/guidelines-tools/regulatory-impact-analysis-statement-low-impact-template.html (accessed 28 June 2017); (Government of Canada, 2014[9]), "Regulatory Impact Analysis Statement (RIAS): Medium-and High-Impact Template", https://www.canada.ca/en/treasury-board-secretariat/services/federal-regulatory-management/guidelines-tools/regulatory-impact-analysis-statement-medium-high-impact-template.html (accessed 28 June 2017).

Box 3.1. Basic questionnaire of the analysis to define the preparation or expansion of RIA in Australia

1. What is the policy problem you are trying to solve?

- Clearly state why the issue being addressed is a problem, emphasising the risks and dangers that can be mitigated by regulation.
- Describe the business, communities and civil organisations being affected by the problem.
- Explain what the government is doing about it (if there is already a policy for this problem) and establish why these measures do not work.

2. Why is government action needed?

- Prove that the government has the capacity to step in and solve the public policy problem.
- Detail the objectives and goals that are set out, including the limitations and barriers to achieve them. The project must be SMART (Specific, Measurable, Achievable, Realistic, Timely).

3. What policy options are you considering?

- Determine feasible and genuine policy options that should be placed in the appropriate political and economic contexts.

4. What is the likely net benefit of each option?
   - Quantify the costs and benefits of the policy proposed that has a bearing on affected actors.
   - Assess the costs and benefits of all the policy options presented as alternatives and analyse the qualitative impacts.
   - Establish the international standards that are carried out in this type of draft proposals.
5. Who will you consult about these options and how will you consult them?
   - The consultation should explain both its purpose and its objectives.
   - Present a plan to carry out the consultation and explain who, and who does not, must participate in it.
   - Build a strategy to ensure that the consultation is as efficient as possible and summarise the main issues that will be addressed.
6. What is the best option among those you have considered?
   - Choose the best option by presenting the exceptions the proposal considers, the assumptions that have been made during the process, the unsolved problems and specific factors in the evidence.
7. How will you implement and assess your chosen option?
   - Present the implementation plan.
   - Assess the risks of the execution and describe how the performance of the regulatory programme will be evaluated during and after its implementation.

Source: Prepared by the OECD, based on (Government of Australia, 2016[2]), "User Guide to the Australian Government Guide to Regulation", https://www.pmc.gov.au/resource-centre/regulation/user-guide-australian-government-guide-regulation (accessed 28 June 2017).

Canada has two types of RIA, low impact and medium-high impact (see Table 3.5). Once the Treasury Board approves the Triage Statement, the regulator should complete the RIA accordingly. The next step in the process to issue regulation is the approval from the Department of Justice and the Regulator in charge. The approval from both agencies allows preparing the first draft of the regulation.

Mexico has two types of RIA for regulations that involve a cost for those subject to regulation, moderate impact and high impact RIAs. In both cases, the assessment is ruled by international best practices. Therefore, it contains six sections: 1) Definition of the problem and general objectives of the regulation; 2) Identification of possible alternatives to the regulation; 3) Impact of the regulation (cost-benefit evaluation); 4) Mechanisms for compliance and enforcement of the proposal; 5) Methodology for the assessment of the proposal (once it is applied); 6) Public consultation. The thoroughness of the analysis, as well as the level of detail in each section, varies according to the type of impact of the regulation.

As in Australia, the European Union has a series of key questions that serve as basis to prepare a RIA (see Table 3.6). The answer to each question is an iterative process that allows identifying the most outstanding and objective information (European Commission,

2009[5]). Moreover, the annexes must include information on the preparation of the impact assessment, a description of the public consultation, as well as a model on the implications of the regulation both in a representative company and in the public administration.

Table 3.6. RIA process in the European Union

Key questions for RIA in the European Union
What is the problem and why is it a problem?
Why must the European Union take action?
What is the expected result?
What options were considered for the accomplishment of the objectives?
What are the economic, social and environmental impacts, and who would be affected?
How do the different options compare in terms of effectiveness and efficiency (costs and benefits)?
How are supervision and *ex post* evaluation going to be carried out?

Source: (European Commission, 2009[5]), "Impact Assessment Guidelines", http://ec.europa.eu/smart-regulation/impact/commission_guidelines/docs/iag_2009_en.pdf (accessed 28 June 2017).

Public consultation

The inclusion of a public consultation on the draft of regulation is a key step of the regulatory governance cycle. OECD countries have included this step into their processes of issuing and reviewing regulation; however, there are still areas of opportunity. In particular, it is necessary to continue working on a mind-set shift, both of the regulators and of those subject to the regulation, so that the parties involved understand the value of the public consultation. In some cases, it is clear that the value of taking this type of measures may be more evident; nevertheless, officials must systematically include citizens, industry and the public sector into the process. The latter not only allows to improve the quality of the regulatory policy but also to increase government transparency and public confidence. The consultation can be carried out through different means and during several periods; it depends, among other things, on the country, the budget and the relevance of the regulation.

The RIA process in Australia involves conducting a public consultation among the individuals, business and organisations affected by the regulation (Government of Australia, 2016[10]). Most of the consultations are open for everyone, except when there are explicit reasons for limiting them, which implies a consultation addressed to a specific audience or a confidential consultation. The Office of Best Practice Regulation establishes that public consultations must be continuous and start as soon as possible in the process to issue regulations. Moreover, they should be addressed to the broadest possible audience and must be easily accessible; it should not impose additional burdens on participants. Finally, consultation should be conducted – but not done hastily –whenever it is necessary to prepare a RIA, in order to make it easier the participation of regulated parties.

In Canada, all subordinate laws require a public consultation before they are passed. Authorities must ensure that the information they provide in the consultations is objective, well-founded, and sets out the steps to be followed. Lastly, the consultation process is open to the largest number of Canadians possible, who should receive feedback from the agency sponsoring the regulation.

In Mexico, once CONAMER approves the RIA, it is mandatory that all regulations be subject to public consultation for a minimum of 30 business days. Calls for consultation should be posted on the websites of the regulators, on the website www.cofemersimir.gob.mx, and social media of CONAMER; and in the federal official gazette (*Diario Oficial de la Federación*, DOF), in the case of technical standards. During the consultation process, public at large and stakeholders are invited to express their opinions, provide information and challenge the analysis. Regulators are obliged to take into account all the comments, which are public, and reply to them.

In the European Union, the public consultation process consists of four key steps:

1. Determining the purpose of the consultation
2. Selecting the interested parties and/or affected ones
3. Choosing the methods and tools to be used (to ensure accessibility), and
4. Creating a webpage linked to the consultation.

The draft regulation has to be available for consultation for four weeks. In particular, the selection of the target audience is determined by a matrix that considers both the influence and the interest of the stakeholders (European Commission, n.d.[11]). According to the quadrant where the highlighted parties are located, it is assigned the priority in the consultation process.

Note

[1] With the publication of the General Law on Regulatory Improvement in May 2018, the former Federal Commission for Regulatory Improvement (COFEMER) converted into the CONAMER.

References

CONAMER (2017), *Portal Gubernamental*, https://www.gob.mx/cofemer (accessed on 28 June 2017). [4]

European Commission (2009), *Impact Assessment Guidelines*, http://ec.europa.eu/smart-regulation/impact/commission_guidelines/docs/iag_2009_en.pdf. [12]

European Commission (2009), *Impact Assessment Guidelines*, http://ec.europa.eu/smart-regulation/impact/commission_guidelines/docs/iag_2009_en.pdf. [5]

European Commission (n.d.), *Tool #50: Stakholder Consultation Tools*, http://ec.europa.eu/smart-regulation/guidelines/tool_50_en.htm. [11]

Government of Australia (2016), *Guidance Note*, https://www.pmc.gov.au/sites/default/files/publications/best-practice-consultation.pdf. [10]

Government of Australia (2016), *User Guide to the Australian Government Guide to Regulation*, https://www.pmc.gov.au/resource-centre/regulation/user-guide-australian-government-guide-regulation (accessed on 26 April 2018). [2]

Government of Canada (2014), *Guide to the Federal Regulatory Development Process*, https://www.canada.ca/en/treasury-board-secretariat/services/federal-regulatory-management/guidelines-tools/guide-federal-regulatory-development-process.html#t1 (accessed on 25 April 2018). [3]

Government of Canada (2014), *Regulatory Impact Analysis Statement (RIAS): Low-Impact Template*, https://www.canada.ca/en/treasury-board-secretariat/services/federal-regulatory-management/guidelines-tools/regulatory-impact-analysis-statement-low-impact-template.html (accessed on 26 April 2018). [8]

Government of Canada (2014), *Regulatory Impact Analysis Statement (RIAS): Medium- and High-Impact Template*, https://www.canada.ca/en/treasury-board-secretariat/services/federal-regulatory-management/guidelines-tools/regulatory-impact-analysis-statement-medium-high-impact-template.html (accessed on 26 April 2018). [9]

Government of Canada (2014), *Triage Statement Form*, https://www.canada.ca/en/treasury-board-secretariat/services/federal-regulatory-management/guidelines-tools/triage-statement-form.html (accessed on 26 April 2018). [7]

OECD (2015), *OECD Regulatory Policy Outlook 2015*, OECD Publishing, Paris, https://dx.doi.org/10.1787/9789264238770-en. [6]

OECD (2012), *Recommendation of the Council on Regulatory Policy and Governance*, OECD Publishing, Paris, http://dx.doi.org/10.1787/9789264209022-en. [1]

Chapter 4. Institutions and legal framework for *ex ante* evaluation of regulations in Peru

This chapter describes and analyses the legal framework applicable to the process to issue regulations in Peru. It also examines the institutions in charge of ensuring the quality of the regulation issued by the Executive of the central government of Peru.

For a number of years, Peru has been making improvements to its legal framework to include international practices in its domestic legislation for adopting tools that contribute to the issuance of quality rules of law, whose main objective is the common good and the promotion of social welfare and economic growth. However, there are still large areas of opportunity to revise the current legal framework and include not only tools but also institutions, and a comprehensive regulatory policy that helps to systematise a process for the issuance of high-quality rules.

This chapter analyses the current regulatory framework, from the Political Constitution of Peru to the latest legal instruments published and that relate to the promotion of quality in regulation. To this end, all applicable regulations are identified and a brief explanation of the objective of each one of them is provided. Also, the analysis covers the institutions from the Executive Branch of the Central Government of Peru involved in the issuance of regulations. Finally, an analysis on how each of them affects the RIA elements, according to the Recommendation of the Council on Regulatory Policy and Governance (OECD, 2012[1]), aims at identifying the progress and needs of Peru regarding regulatory quality.

Current legal framework

Table 4.1 shows the legal instruments related to the *ex ante* evaluation of regulations in Peru. A brief description of each of them is presented below.

- Political Constitution of Peru (*Constitución Política del Perú*)

The supreme instrument of the Peruvian legal system that states the human, economic, political and social rights of the Peruvian State; consequently, it prevails over all other legal rules.

This instrument lays down, initially, the importance of publicity for the legal force of all State rules;[1] as well as the regulatory powers of the President of the Republic to issue decrees and resolutions.[2]

- Law N° 26889: Framework Law for Legislative Production and Systematization (*Ley* N° *26889: Ley Marco para la Producción y Sistematización Legislativa*)

Law that lays down guidelines to prepare, title, and publish laws. This law aims to systematise and give coherence to the national legislation.

- Law N° 27444: Law of General Administrative Procedure (*Ley* N° 27444: *Ley de Procedimiento Administratrivo General*)

Law that establishes the rules that must be observed by the entities of the Executive in their administrative duties. This law governs all administrative procedures developed in the entities and establishes the applicable legal regime so that the acts of the public administration protect the general interest, guarantee the rights and interests of regulated parties and be subject to the constitutional and legal system, in general.[3] To this end, the 16 principles on which the administrative procedure is based are established. The concept of administrative action is also established.[4]

Table 4.1. Current legal framework that has a bearing on regulations in Peru

Title	Nº	Year of publication
1. Political Constitution of Peru (*Constitución Política del Perú*)		Dec. 1993
2. Framework Law for Legislative Production and Systematization (*Ley Marco para la Producción y Sistematización Legislativa*)	26889	Dec. 1997
3. Law of the General Administrative Procedure (*Ley de Procedimiento Administrativo General*)	27444	Apr. 2001
4. Law on Transparency and Access to Public Information (*Ley de Transparencia y Acceso a la Información Pública*)	27806	Apr. 2003
5. Organic Law of the Executive Branch (*Ley Orgánica del Poder Ejecutivo*)	29158	Dec. 2007
6. Bylaw of the Framework Law for Legislative Production and Systematization (*Reglamento de la Ley Marco para la Producción y Sistematización Legislativa*)	008-2006-JUS	Mar.2006
7. Supreme Decree approving the bylaw that lays down rules on advertising, publication of regulatory proposals, and dissemination of general legal rules *(Decreto Supremo que aprueba el Reglamento que establece las disposiciones relativas a la publicidad, publicación de proyectos normativos y difusión de normas legales de carácter general*)	001-2009-JUS	Jan. 2009
8. Guide on Legislative Technique for the Development of Regulatory Proposals from the Entities of the Executive Branch (*Guía de Técnica Legislativa para la elaboración de Proyectos Normativos de las Entidades del Poder Ejecutivo*)	007-2016-JUS/DGDOJ	Jun.2016
9. Legislative decree approving additional measures of administrative simplification (*Decreto Legislativo que aprueba medidas adicionales de Simplificación administrativa*)	1310	Dec. 2016
10. Supreme Decree that approves the Bylaw for the application of the Regulatory Quality Analysis of administrative procedures provided for in Article 2 of Legislative Decree Nº 1310 (*Decreto Supremo que aprueba el Reglamento para la aplicación del Análisis de Calidad Regulatoria de procedimientos administrativos establecido en el artículo 2 del Decreto Legislativo Nº 1310*)	075-2017-PCM	Jul.2017
11. Ministerial Resolution that approves the Manual for the application of the Regulatory Quality Analysis (*Resolución Ministerial que aprueba el Manual para la aplicación del Análisis de Calidad Regulatoria*)	196-2017-PCM	Aug.2017
12. Resolution that approves the Documentary Management Model within the framework of the Legislative Decree Nº 1310 (*Resolución que aprueba el Modelo de Gestión Documental en el Marco del Decreto Legislativo Nº 1310*)	001-2017-PCM/SEGDI	Aug.2017
13. Ministerial Resolution, Internal Bylaw of the Multisectoral Commission of Regulatory Quality (*Resolución Ministerial, Reglamento Interno de la Comisión Multisectorial de Calidad Regulatoria*)	199-2017-PCM	Aug. 2017
14. Supreme Decree approving the Bylaw of Organization and Functions of the Presidency of the Council of Ministers (*Decreto Supremo que aprueba el Reglamento de Organización y Funciones de la Presidencia del Consejo de Ministros*)	022-2017-PCM	Feb.2017
15. Legislative Decree that modifies Article 2 of the Legislative Decree Nº 1310, Legislative Decree approving additional measures of administrative simplification and perfects the institutional framework and the instruments that rule the process of regulatory improvement(*Decreto Legislativo que modifica el Artículo 2 del Decreto Legislativo Nº 1310, Decreto Legislativo que aprueba medidas adicionales de simplificación administrativa y perfecciona el marco institucional y los instrumentos que rigen el proceso de mejora de calidad regulatoria*)	1448	Sep. 2018
16. Legislative Decree that modifies the Law Nº 27444, Law of General Administrative Procedure (*Decreto Legislativo que modifica la Ley Nº 27444, Ley de Procedimiento Administrativo General*)	1452	Sep. 2018

- Law Nº 27806: Law on Transparency and Access to Public Information (*Ley Nº 27806: Ley de Transparencia y Acceso a la Información Pública*)

The purpose of this law is to promote transparency in the acts of the State and regulate the right of regulated parties to access public information.[5] This law lays down the obligation for entities of the Public Administration of disseminating various provisions and statements on their websites; thereby, transparency of their acts and the access to information are promoted.

- Law N° 29158: Organic Law of the Executive Branch (*Ley N° 29158: Ley Orgánica del Poder Ejecutivo*)

Law establishing the principles and basic rules for the organisation, powers and duties of the Executive Branch, composed of the President of the Republic, the Council of Ministers, the Presidency of the Council of Ministers, the ministries and the public entities of the Executive Power, as part of the national government.

This law lays down the statutory functions of the Executive Branch,[6] the legislative tasks of the President of the Republic[7] and his/her rule-making powers, the concepts of the different regulatory instruments the President can issue,[8] such as legislative decrees, supreme decrees, supreme resolutions, among others, as well as the process this regulatory power will be subject to.[9]

Moreover, in includes the rule-making powers of the president of the Council of Ministers,[10] the ministries[11] and deputy ministers.[12]

- Bylaw of the Framework Law for Legislative Production and Systematization – DS. N° 008-2006-JUS (*Reglamento de la Ley Marco para la Producción y Sistematización Legislativa – DS. N° 008-2006-JUS*)

It elaborates on the provisions of Law N° 26889 related to the structure that must be observed to prepare, title, and publish national legislation.

This bylaw applies to the preparation of bills, draft of legislative, emergency and supreme decrees;[13] and it lays out the guidelines on legislative technique aimed at harmonising the texts of normative provisions, contributing to improve its quality and legal certainty.[14]

This instrument provides for, among other elements, a cost-benefit analysis and an analysis of the impact of the life of the rule on national legislation.[15]

- Bylaw that lays down rules on advertising, publication of regulatory proposals, and dissemination of general legal rules (Reglamento que establece disposiciones relativas a la publicidad, publicación de proyectos normativos y difusión de normas legales de carácter general).

Bylaw that lays down the mandatory publication of general legal rules,[16] as well as the pre-publication in the *Official Gazette El Peruano*, and the receipt of comments from the interested parties. Furthermore, it promotes the permanent dissemination of these legal rules on the websites of the public entities from the Executive Branch and by means of other institutional tools.[17]

This instrument lays down the concept of general legal rule and, consequently, the sets of laws that must obligatorily be published, in the *Official Gazette El Peruano*,[18] which, by failing to comply with this obligation, will become ineffective and null.[19]

- Guide on Legislative Technique for the Development of Regulatory Proposals from the Entities of the Executive Branch (*Guía de Técnica Legislativa para la elaboración de Proyectos Normativos de las Entidades del Poder Ejecutivo*)

This practical guide aims to direct, in a simple way, the organic units of the Executive Branch in charge of developing regulatory proposals, to help in the performance of their duties.

The legislative capability of the President of the Republic is reaffirmed through the issuance of legislative and emergency decrees,[20] as well as his/her rule-making power,[21] which he/she exercises by him/herself and through the public entities and agencies composing the Executive Branch.

- Legislative Decree N° 1310 approving additional measures of administrative simplification (*Decreto Legislativo N° 1310 que aprueba medidas adicionales de simplificación administrativa*)

Decree laying out administrative simplification measures that, unlike the previous instruments, establishes the obligation of conducting a regulatory quality analysis to all general normative provisions issued by the Executive Branch that lay down administrative procedures (formalities). It aims to identify, reduce and/or eliminate those formalities that are unnecessary, unjustified, disproportionate, inefficient, redundant, or that are inconsistent with the laws that support them.[22]

The Decree creates the Multisectoral Commission of Regulatory Quality (*Comisión Multisectorial de Calidad Regulatoria*), which is presided by the PCM. The regulatory quality analysis will be validated by a Multisectoral Commission, where the MINJUSDH and MEF also participate.

Moreover, this decree lay down the obligation for public administration entities to interconnect their systems of documentary procedure or equivalent for the automatic transmission of electronic documents through the State Interoperability Platform (PIDE).[23]

The implementation of the Regulatory Quality Analysis (RQA) represents an important step in the adoption of an *ex ante* evaluation system of the regulation in Peru. Box 4.1 contains a more detailed description of the RQA. In relation to this decree, and for its proper functioning, the following regulatory instruments were emitted:

- DS. 022-2017-PCM: Supreme Decree approving the Bylaw of Organization and Functions of the Presidency of the Council of Ministers (*DS. 022-2017-PCM: Decreto Supremo que aprueba el Reglamento de Organización y Funciones de la Presidencia del Consejo de Ministros*)

Bylaw laying down the duties of the Presidency of the Council of Ministers as the body responsible for the co-ordination of the domestic policies from the Executive Branch,[24] with authority over the modernisation of the State management and digital government, as well as with the task of promoting the quality of the regulations emitted by the public administration.

With this decree, the Under-secretariat for Simplification and Regulatory Analysis[25] is created, within the Secretariat of Public Management. This Under secretariat's duties include topics on administrative simplification of formalities, regulatory quality and the analysis of the RQA.

- Bylaw for the application of the Regulatory Quality Analysis of Administrative Procedures provided for in Article 2 of Legislative Decree N° 1310 (*Reglamento para la aplicación del Análisis de Calidad Regulatoria de Procedimientos Administrativos establecido en el Artículo 2 del Decreto Legislativo N° 1310*)

This bylaw lays down guidelines and statutory provisions to promote the quality in regulation.[26] For such purpose, this bylaw establishes a definition of Regulatory Quality Analysis,[27] as well as of the regulatory instruments it should be applied to,[28] those that are excluded,[29] and the principles that must be evaluated when carrying out the analysis.[30]

The bylaw also establishes the accountable parties of this analysis: Secretary General of the Executive Branch,[31] the Multisectoral Commission[32] and Technical Secretariat,[33] laying out the tasks of each of these actors in this process.

- RM. 199-2017-PCM: Ministerial Resolution N° 199-2017-PCM, Internal Bylaw of the Multisectoral Commission of Regulatory Quality (RM. 199-2017-PCM: *Resolución Ministerial N° 199-2017-PCM, Reglamento Interno de la Comisión Multisectorial de Calidad Regulatoria*)

This bylaw aims to establish the conditions of organisation[34] and operation[35] for the Multisectoral Commission of Regulatory Quality.

- RM. 196-2017-PCM: Ministerial Resolution N° 196-2017-PCM that approves the Manual for the application of the Regulatory Quality Analysis (*RM. 196-2017-PCM*: *Resolución Ministerial* N° 196-2017-PCM *a través de la cual se aprueba el Manual para la aplicación del Análisis de Calidad Regulatoria*)

This manual contains the applicable criteria to prepare and assess the Regulatory Quality Analysis of regulations producing administrative formalities, as well as the methodology for its assessment and the forms that should be filled in for their submission and processing.

This manual lays down the different types of quality regulation analysis that will be employed for the different normative provisions, as well as the effects that each type will have.[36]

- DL. N° 1448: Legislative Decree N° 1448 that modifies Article 2 of the Legislative Decree N° 1310, Legislative Decree that approves the additional administrative simplification measures and perfects the institutional framework and the instruments that rule the process of improvement of regulatory quality (*DL N°1448: Decreto Legislativo N° 1448 que modifica el Artículo 2 del Decreto Legislativo N°1310, Decreto Legislativo que aprueba medidas adicionales de simplificación administrative, y perfecciona el marco institucional y los instrumentos que rigen el proceso de mejora de calidad regulatoria*)

This Decree modifies and improves the RQA system. This Decree introduces new articles that refer to "The improvement of regulatory quality", and the tools to improve the quality of regulations. The former include, among others, the *ex ante* and *ex post* regulatory impact analysis. Moreover, the decree establishes the obligation for the PCM, MEF and MINJUSDH to pass a decree that approves the RIA.

With these new articles, Peru establishes the bases for the adoption of a regulatory policy and the RIA.

- DL. N°1452: Legislative Decree N°1452, which modifies the Law N°27444, Law of General Administrative Procedure (*DL N°1452: Decreto Legislativo N°1452, que modifica la Ley N°27444, Ley de Procedimiento Administrativo General*)

The decree establishes several modifications to the Law of General Administrative Procedure with regards to topics such as negative administrative silence as a legal figure that can be applied exceptionally, the creation of administrative procedures in a high-level legal instrument and more requirements for formalities of renovation of authorisations, standardised administrative procedures, improvements to the Unique Text of Administrative Procedures (TUPA), among others. In relation to the RQA, the decree defines that the PCM has the authority to emit a preliminary favourable opinion for the approval of the TUPA of the entities of the Executive Branch once the RQA stage is concluded, they are forced to update the TUPA and upload the procedures to the Unique System of Formalities (SUT).

- RS. 001-2017-PCM/SEGDI: Resolution N° 001-2017-PCM/SEGDI. The Documentary Management Model is approved by virtue of Legislative Decree N° 1310 that approves additional administrative simplification measures (*RS. 001-2017-PCM/SEGDI: Resolución N° 001-2017-PCM/SEGDI. Aprueban Modelo de Gestión Documental en el marco del Decreto Legislativo N° 1310 que aprueba medidas adicionales de simplificación administrativa*).

This regulatory instrument aims to approve the Documentary Management Model, as the widespread-use model within the public administration for the automatic transmission of electronic documents, as provided for in Article 8 of Legislative Decree N° 1310.

Box 4.1. Types of Regulatory Quality Analysis in Peru

The Regulatory Quality Analysis (RQA) was introduced by the Legislative Decree N° 1310, published on December 30, 2016 in the Official Gazette El Peruano. Afterwards, the Legislative Decree N°1448 published on September 16, 2018 modified the Legislative Decree N°1310 and included additional legal specifications.

According to the Legislative Decree N° 1448 "The entities of the Executive Branch must carry out a Regulatory Quality Analysis of the administrative procedures established in the legal dispositions of general scope with the intention of identifying, eliminating and/or simplifying those that are deemed unnecessary, unjustified, disproportionate, redundant or are not adequate according to the Law of General Administrative Procedure or the norms with the same hierarchical level as a law that support them."

Furthermore, the Legislative Decree N° 1448 mentions that "one of the objectives of the Regulatory Quality Analysis is to identify and reduce the administrative burdens that regulated parties face as a consequence of the formality of the administrative procedure".

According to these decrees, and to the Supreme Decree N° 022-2017-PCM that establishes the Bylaw for the application of the RQA, the RQA is a tool with the purpose of improving the quality of the regulatory flow and of the regulatory stock. Table 4.2 shows the different types of RQA.

Regarding the regulatory flow, the government entities that are forced to prepare a RQA in case they want to emit new norms or modify an existing one, and that contain administrative procedures, with the exceptions of laws or norms with the same hierarchical level as a law, which could be considered a RQA *ex ante*. The RQA must be reviewed by the Multisectoral Commission of Regulatory Quality.

The Multisectoral Commission of Regulatory Quality, presided by the Secretary General of the PCM, and that includes the participation of the Vice minister of economy of the MEF and the Vice minister of Justice of the MINJUSDH, or their representatives.

Regarding the regulatory stock, the entities of the government are required to prepare a RQA for the current regulation that includes administrative procedures, with the exception of laws or norms with the same hierarchical level as laws, which could be considered as a RQA of the normative stock. This RQA must be also subject to the revision of the Multisectoral Commission of Regulatory Quality, and thus, they are ratified or eliminated by the Council of Ministers. The RQA Guidelines published by the PCM develops the principles (legality, need, effectiveness and proportionality) through a series of questions to evaluate the formalities and the Supreme Decree 022-2017-PCM has a calendar for the delivery of the RQA for the entities of the government. One of the objectives of the RQA is to create a baseline measurement of the administrative burden of the formalities in the Executive Branch with the objective of establishing reduction goals.

Once the Multisectoral Commission of Regulatory Improvement validates the RQA, the entities are required to prepare a new RQA of the validated procedures three years after their approval date and submit it to the Multisectoral Commission of Regulatory Improvement and to the Council of Ministers.

As a response, the Multisectoral Commission of Regulatory Improvement emits a report on the rules and procedures that may be ratified or issued and will be in force for a period not exceeding three years; and those not ratified will automatically be repealed. The lists of ratified normative provisions are published in the official gazette by means of supreme decrees, for dissemination, and they are approved by the Council of Ministers. Effectively, the Multisectoral Commission of Regulatory Improvement has the authority to reject the RQA that are not adequate and to propose the elimination of administrative procedures that do not comply with the established criteria.

Table 4.2. Types of Regulatory Quality Analysis and their effects

TYPE OF RQA	NORMATIVE DISPOSITIONS	EFFECTS OF THE RQA	
		VALIDATED BY THE CCR*	NOT VALIDATED BY THE CCR
RQA OF THE STOCK	Normative provisions in force that lay down administrative procedures	They are ratified by means of Supreme Decree, approved by the Council of Ministers, for a term not exceeding 3 years	Those that have not been expressly ratified by the Council of Ministers are automatically repealed
EX ANTE RQA	Draft of new normative provisions that lay down administrative procedures Modification drafts of normative provisions in force that lay down administrative procedures	They continue with the process of approval by the entity for the issuance of the corresponding instrument	They do not continue with the process of approval and cannot be approved until the CCR validates them
RQA of Validated Administrative Procedures (3 years)	Normative provisions that lay down administrative procedures, before the expiration of the 3-year period of being ratified or issued	They are ratified by means of Supreme Decree, approved by the Council of Ministers, for a term not exceeding 3 years	They are automatically repealed if, after the expiration of a 3-year period of being ratified or issued, they have not been expressly ratified by the Council of Ministers

Source: Adapted from the Supreme Decree approving the Bylaw of Organization and Functions of the Presidency of the Council of Ministers (*Decreto Supremo que aprueba el Reglamento de Organización y Funciones de la Presidencia del Consejo de Ministros*) (DS. 022-2017-PCM, 2017), Bylaw for the application of the Regulatory Quality Analysis of administrative procedures laid down in Article 2 of Legislative Decree N° 1310 (*Reglamento para la aplicación del Análisis de Calidad Regulatoria de Procedimientos Administrativos establecido en el Artículo 2 del Decreto Legislativo N° 1310) (DS. 075-2017-PCM, 2017*) and Ministerial Resolution N° 196-2017-PCM that approves the Manual for the application of the Regulatory Quality Analysis (*Resolución Ministerial N° 196-2017-PCM a través de la cual se aprueba el Manual para la aplicación del Análisis de Calidad Regulatoria*) (RM. 196-2017-PCM), http://sgp.pcm.gob.pe/wp-content/uploads/2017/08/Manual-Analisis-de-Calidad-Regulatoria.pdf.

Institutions

Peru has some government agencies with tasks directly related to the promotion of quality in regulation. Table 4.3 shows the agencies involved in this process.

Table 4.3. Government organisations and institutions with crosscutting tasks in the process to issue regulations in Peru

Organisations
Presidency of the Council of Ministers
Vice-Ministerial Coordinating Council
Ministry of Justice and of Human Rights
Ministry of Economy and Finance
Multisectoral Commission of Regulatory Quality

- Presidency of the Council of Ministers (PCM)

It is responsible for co-ordinating domestic sectoral and multisectoral policies from the Executive Branch, as well as the relations with some other branches, autonomous bodies, subnational governments, and civil society. Furthermore, it is the governing body of the Administrative System for the Modernization of Public Management,[37] which promotes public management-wide reforms applicable to all entities and levels of government,[38] empowered to handle matters of operation and organisation of the State, administrative simplification, ethics and transparency, citizen participation and the promotion of regulatory quality[39] among others.

The Secretariat of Public Management, subordinated to the General Secretariat,[40] is in charge of the management of this System. In order to fulfil its duties, this Secretariat has the Under-secretariat for Simplification and Regulatory Assessment, among other bodies.

The tasks of this Under-secretariat focus, primarily, on administrative simplification issues and regulatory quality, including:

- Design, elaborate, update, propose and implement policies, plans and strategies regarding administrative simplification and actions on regulatory quality.
- Elaborate reports with the opinions required by the Law in terms of administrative simplification, exclusive services and regulatory quality.
- Supervise and verify the compliance with the norms related to administrative simplification and regulatory quality
- Design and propose indicators and tools that facilitate the tracking and evaluation of the plans and other instruments linked to administrative simplification and regulatory quality.

Also, it is in charge of implementing methodologies and actions for the regulatory impact assessment of formalities in the process of elaboration of norms and provide opinions and guidance to other public entities with regards to the use of the Regulatory Impact Assessment in the process of elaboration of norms.[41] This Under secretariat is responsible for the Technical Secretariat that provides specialised support to the CCR in the process of analysis of the regulatory quality.

- Vice-Ministerial Coordinating Council (CCV)

This body is subordinated to the General Secretariat of the Presidency of the Council of Ministers. CCV is comprised by the deputy ministers from the Executive Branch and the Secretary General of the PCM,[42] who is responsible for convening and presiding over it.

Its objective is to co-ordinate multisectoral issues among deputy ministers,[43] whenever a general legal instrument is intended to be issued, that involves more than two ministries or that requires the approval vote of the Council of Ministers, this shall be approved by the CCV, which generates a relevant normative co-ordination and control mechanism; its intervention. However, is only for this type of administrative acts of general multisectoral nature. Consequently, in the cases where only one or two ministries are involved, this control body does not participate.

- Ministry of Justice and Human Rights (MINJUSDH)

According to the specific tasks stated in the Law on Organization and Functions of the Ministry of Justice[44] and Human Rights and its Bylaw,[45] the MINJUSDH is the body in charge of providing legal advice to the Executive Branch on regulatory proposals, as well as of promoting regulatory coherence via the consistent enforcement of the Peruvian legal system. Moreover, in the event of differences among the legal opinions issued by the legal advice units of the entities from the Executive Branch, this Ministry will be the one that establish the prevailing opinion, promoting thus regulatory coherence.

These tasks are carried out through the General Directorate of Policy Development and Regulatory Quality[46] which, in turn, counts on the Directorate of Legal Development and Regulatory Quality as one of its organisational units,[47] and who performs more specific tasks in terms of regulatory quality and coherence.[48]

- Ministry of Economy and Finance (MEF)

According to its Bylaw of Organization and Functions, the MEF has capability, among other issues, to harmonise the national economic and financial activity to promote its competitiveness, the continuous improvement of productivity, and the efficient operation of markets.[49]

It has two vice-ministerial offices, Treasury and Economy.[50] Among other tasks, the Economy office co-ordinates, executes and supervises the application of policies, strategies, plans, programs, and projects of microeconomic nature, including – among others – productivity matters.[51] This vice-ministry has various entities to discharge its duties; one of them is the General Directorate of International Economy, Competition and Productivity Affairs,[52] in charge of proposing, directing and preparing policy measures, among others, in the domain of regulatory quality. As well as ensuring the consistency of the economic integration processes with the general economic policy, in order to promote continuous increases in productivity and competitiveness in the country.[53]

This General Directorate has the Directorate of Normative Efficiency for Productivity and Competition which is responsible for, among other tasks, evaluating the regulatory impact of provisions – issued by the State – that create distortions in the market and affect free competition, in order to prevent efficiency losses in the allocation of resources and operation of markets.[54]

- Multisectoral Commission of Regulatory Quality (CCR)

This Commission was created pursuant to Article 2 of Legislative Decree N° 1310, and its Internal Rules was issued through Ministerial Resolution 199-2017-PCM.

It consists of three actors: the PCM, through the Secretary General, who presides over it, and the Under-secretariat for Administrative Simplification and Regulatory Analysis, who acts as the Technical Secretary of the Commission; the MEF, through the Deputy Minister of Economy; and the MINJUSDH, through the Deputy Minister of Justice.[55]

The purpose of this Commission is to validate the regulatory quality analysis that must be prepared by the entities of the Executive Branch[56] to their regulation that establishes administrative procedures or formalities; to issue the corresponding reports regarding the rules and procedures that are duly justified, and to propose their ratification by the Council of Ministers or their issuance by the relevant entity.[57]

Notes

[1] Art. 51. Political Constitution of Peru.

[2] Art. 118. Political Constitution of Peru.

[3] Art. III. – Purpose. Law N° 27444.

[4] Art. 1. - Concept of Administrative Action. 1.1 Administrative actions are the statements of entities that, within the framework of public-law rules, are aimed to produce legal effects on the interests, obligations or rights of regulated parties in a specific situation. Law N° 27444.

[5] Art. 1. - Scope of the Law. Law N° 27806.

[6] Art. 6. - Duties of the Executive Branch. Law N° 29158.

[7] Art. 8. - Duties of the President of the Republic. Law N° 29158.

[8] Art. 11. - Rule-making power of the President of the Republic. Law N° 29158.

[9] Art. 13. - Regulatory power. Law N° 29158.

[10] Art. 19. - 9. Law N° 29158.

[11] Art. 23.- 23.1, b). Law N° 29158.

[12] Art. 26.- 3. Law N° 29158.

[13] Art. I. Scope of application. DS. 008-2006-JUS.

[14] Art. II. Purpose. DS. 008-2006-JUS.

[15] Art. 1. - Parts of the regulatory structure. DS. 008-2006-JUS.

[16] Art. 1. - Subject matter of the Bylaw. DS. 001-2009-JUS.

[17] Art. 14. - Dissemination of draft general legal rules. DS. 001-2009-JUS.

[18] Art. 4. - Scope of the concept of the legal rules. DS. 001-2009-JUS.

[19] Art. 7. Compulsory disclosure of legal rules. DS. 001-2009-JUS.

[20] Chapter I. General aspects. 1.2. The power of the President of the Republic to issue legal status rules.

[21] Chapter I. General aspects. 1.3. The regulatory power of the Executive Branch.

[22] Art. 2. - Regulatory Quality Analysis of administrative procedures. DL. 1310.

[23] Art. 8. - Systems of Documentary Procedure of Public Administration Entities. DL. 1310.

[24] Art. 2. - Powers. 2.1. DS. 022-2017-PCM.

[25] Art. 6. - Presidency of the Council of Ministers 06 Line bodies. 06.3 Secretariat of Public Management. 06.3.2. Under-secretariat for Simplification and Regulatory Analysis. DS. 022-2017-PCM.

[26] Art. 1. - Purpose. DS. 075-2017-PCM.

[27] Art. 3. - Definitions. 3.2. Regulatory Quality Analysis DS.075-2017-PCM.

[28] Art. 4. - Normative provisions included in the Regulatory Quality Analysis by the Entities of the Executive Branch. DS. 075-2017-PCM.

[29] Final supplementary provisions.

[30] Art. 5. - The principles that are evaluated in the regulatory quality analysis. DS. 075-2017-PCM.

[31] Art. 6. - Official in charge of conducting and sending the Regulatory Quality Analysis. DS 075-2017-PCM.

[32] Art. 7. - Multisectoral Commission of Regulatory Quality DS. 075-2017-PCM.

[33] Art. 10. - Technical Secretariat. DS. 075-2017-PCM.

[34] Title II. Organization of the Multisectoral Commission of Regulatory Quality RM. 199-2017-PCM.

[35] Title III. Functions. RM. 199-2017-PCM.

[36] Box 4.1. Types of RQA and its effects. RM. 196-2017-PCM.

[37] Art. 2. - Powers. DS. 022-2017-PCM.

[38] Política Nacional de Modernización de la Gestión Pública al 2021 (National Policy for the Modernization of Public Management to 2021), p. 67. http://sgp.pcm.gob.pe/wp-content/uploads/2017/04/PNMGP.pdf.

[39] Art 3-h, Bylaw of Organisation and Functions of the Presidency of the Council of Ministers.

[40] Art. 41. - Secretariat of Public Management. DS. 022-2017-PCM.

[41] Art. 45 Functions of the Under Secretariat of Administrative Simplification and Regulatory Assessment. DS. 022-2017-PCM.

[42] Art 26.- Vice-ministers. LOPE.

[43] Art. 2. - Purpose of the Vice-Ministerial Coordination Council RM. 251-2013-PCM.

[44] Art. 7. - Specific functions. Law N° 29809.

[45] Art. 5, 5. 2- Specific functions. DS. 013-2017-JUS.

[46] Art. 54. - Functions of the General Directorate of Policy Development and Regulatory Quality. DS. 013-2017-JUS.

[47] Art. 55. - Organizational units of the General Directorate of Policy Development and Regulatory Quality. DS. 013-2017-JUS.

[48] Art. 56. - Functions of the Directorate of Legal Development and Regulatory Quality. DS. 013-2017-JUS.

[49] Art. 2. - Powers. DS. 117-2014-EF.

[50] Art. 5. - Organizational Structure. DS. 117-2014-EF.

[51] Art. 12, b). - Functions of the Deputy Minister of Economy. DS. 117-2014-EF.

[52] Art. 13, 5. Entities subordinated to the Vice-Ministerial Office of Economy. DS. 117-2014-EF.

[53] Art. 139. - General Directorate of International Economy, Competition and Productivity Affairs. DS. 117-2014-EF.

[54] Art. 143. - Functions of the Directorate of Normative Efficiency for Productivity and Competition. DS. 117-2014-EF.

[55] Art. 3. - Multisectoral Commission of Regulatory Quality RM. 199-2017-PCM.

[56] Art. 7. - Multisectoral Commission of Regulatory Quality DS. 075-2017-PCM.

[57] Art. 9. - Functions of the Multisectoral Commission of Regulatory Quality DS. 075-2017-PCM.

Reference

OECD (2012), *Recommendation of the Council on Regulatory Policy and Governance*, OECD Publishing, Paris, http://dx.doi.org/10.1787/9789264209022-en. [1]

Chapter 5. The regulation issuing process in Peru

In this chapter, the process to issue regulations followed by five ministries of Peru is thoroughly analysed and compared with the practices of regulatory impact assessment, according to the OECD countries' standards.

The main objective of this review is to support the Peruvian government in the adoption of RIA as a tool to ensure the quality of the regulation that it issues, either for new proposals or to modify the existing ones. Before identifying and assessing the current process to issue regulations in Peru, it is necessary to identify the most common elements used by the OECD countries in the RIA process and, thus, be able to make a comparison with the process followed in Peru.

Good RIA practices in OECD countries

Table 5.1 shows a list of the most common elements found in the RIA systems of OECD countries. Taken together, they represent the good practices for the *ex ante* analysis of regulations. Their importance and relevance are briefly explained below and more detailed in Chapter 7.

Table 5.1. Essential stages of the regulatory impact assessment

Building block
Definition of the problem
Public policy objectives
Alternatives to the regulation
Impact evaluation: cost-benefit analysis
Compliance with regulation
Monitoring and evaluation
Public consultation

Definition of the problem

Defining the existing problem is the first step of the RIA and, consequently, of the process to issue regulations. Insofar as the problem is properly identified – its dimensions and origin – it will be possible to design instruments that reduce or eliminate the risks. A poorly identified problem is the prelude to misguided policies and substandard results, at best. Undoubtedly, the identification of the problem is the most important step of any regulatory impact assessment.

Public policy objectives

Once the problem is identified – the possible effects and consequences – and that government intervention is justified, the RIA should set out specific goals aimed to solve the causes of the problem in question.

A very common mistake is confusing "means" and "ends". The regulatory objective is the "final result" that the government wants to achieve. This should not be confused with the "means" to achieve it because, otherwise, it excludes all the alternatives that may exist. For instance, a public policy objective may be to reduce the number of deaths due to traffic accidents, reducing the speed limit is a means to achieve the goal, but it is not the goal itself. Other means may be to require particular safety measures or to improve road conditions. This example shows that there are several ways and options to achieve the goal.

Alternatives to the regulation

In many cases, the initial analysis done through the RIA may indicate that regulating is not the best option. Some other type of tool can allow to achieve the goals we pursue in a more efficient and effective way. In those cases, the RIA can help, for it gives more insight into the possible impacts of alternative approaches to regulation to achieve public policy objectives. On the other hand, the analysis may reveal that the government intervention is not necessary.

RIA can conclude that the status quo may be the more efficient approach to solve the problem, this can occur in the following cases:

- When the size of the problem is so small that the costs of government action are not justified, and
- When the analysis proves that a rule, or any other action, is not feasible to address effectively the problem at a reasonable cost, thus not getting a positive benefit.

Impact evaluation: cost-benefit analysis

The information about costs and benefits can be of two types: quantitative and qualitative (see Box 7.7 and Box 7.8 for a brief explanation of the methodologies). Quantitative information is expressed in numerical terms, and sometimes in monetary ones. It is the most useful for decision makers, as it allows them to weigh the magnitude of the benefits and costs – analysed and expressed in monetary terms – , when comparing the impact of the different alternatives.

This means that quantitative information should be obtained –insofar as possible –about the size of the problem, the costs of regulatory action, and the expected benefits. In many cases, however, it is impossible to determine the monetary terms for the quantitative analysis. Then, qualitative information can also be part of the analysis. It is important to present the information as clearly and objectively as possible; for, those who read the analysis could interpret in different ways the qualitative information of a potential problem.

The cost-benefit analysis can be considered both as a decision-making guide and as a typical methodology of RIA. The analysis should be the basis for all RIAs of high-impact regulations. This would help ensure the regulation is only issued when the benefits are greater than the costs it imposes.

As a methodology, the cost-benefit analysis represents the best practice to conduct a RIA. In fact, the OECD Recommendation of the Council on Regulatory Policy and Governance established that member countries and associates of the OECD should "adopt practices of *ex ante* impact assessment that are proportional to the regulation and include a cost-benefit analysis that takes into account the impact of the regulation the wellbeing" (OECD, 2012[1]). The cost-benefit analysis provides a sound basis to compare alternatives and guide decisions among several options, for the quantification of benefits and costs in monetary terms and the comparison over a certain period backs it up.

Compliance with regulation

An important element of evaluating impacts is to make a realistic analysis of the compliance rate that is expected to be achieved with the draft proposal. The regulation will only have an impact if people comply with it.

In general, if compliance rates tend to be low, it is essential to be able to detect or reduce noncompliance through implementation actions. If not possible, then a failure in regulation may occur. It means reconsidering the regulatory proposal and check if there is an alternative mechanism that could be more effective.

Monitoring and evaluation

The monitoring and evaluation of the regulatory proposal will make it possible to clearly identify if the public policy objectives are being achieved, as well as to determine if the proposed regulation is needed or how can it be more effective and efficient to reach the stated objectives.

From the very moment the regulation is designed, the mechanisms to be used should also be devised; which, therefore, must be implemented to monitor if compliance with regulation leads to accomplish the objectives set out in the beginning. Likewise, the mechanisms that will be created to make an evaluation of the performance of regulations – also known as *ex post* evaluation – , should be foreseen. The *ex post* evaluation will allow to determine if the regulation contributed to solve the identified problem and, therefore, to accomplish the public policy objective.

Public consultation

One of the most effective ways to obtain information that supports the RIA is to consult potentially affected groups. Furthermore, consultation helps to legitimise regulation because people is able to question and participate in the regulatory process before the regulation is enforced. In this way, voluntary compliance with regulation can increase.

Although consultation is an effective way to obtain information and data to prepare the RIA, it is also necessary to provide enough information to support the consultation process itself. People will participate more fully in the consultation if they know the regulatory proposal and the problem intended to be solved. Written materials explaining all this must be made available to the groups in advance, so they can read and analyse them. Specific questions can be devised to help getting information about concrete subjects. The consultation process should be open enough for groups to express their doubts. Thanks to this, the process will be better accepted by all and, in some cases, it may alert about possible problems that have not been widely considered.

The timing for consultation is also relevant. First, carrying out consultation should be as soon as possible and at various times of the regulatory process so that the results are efficiently used in the RIA or, potentially, lead to changes in the regulatory proposal. Second, it must be ensured that groups have enough time to consult and, in fact, to participate.

In the long term, people will participate in the consultation if they feel it is worth doing so. That means that their opinions should be taken into account during the regulatory process. Replying to their questions or doubts is a good way to maintain the spirit of the participants. The responses to the consultation must be posted on the Internet, along with the details of the government's reaction to the opinions.

Process to issue regulations in Peru

In order to identify the legal provisions, the institutional rules and the current practices on the *ex ante* evaluation of regulatory proposals in Peru, a mapping of what could be considered the regulatory governance cycle in the country was carried out for a group of ministries. This mapping is exclusively for the 2014-16 period, it does not includes the ACR evaluation.[1] However, the changes to the mapping of the regulatory governance cycle in the five selected ministries brought about by the introduction of the ACR are considered at the end of this chapter.

As mentioned above, the regulatory governance cycle is a process by which the government identifies a public policy problem and decides to address it by enforcing an instrument in particular, which should be assessed before being issued. These are the five ministries selected for analysing their process to issue regulations:[2]

- Ministry of Economy and Finance
- Ministry of Production
- Ministry of Environment
- Ministry of Transport and Communications
- Ministry of Housing, Construction and Sanitation

Each of the processes shown and analysed below was created from in-depth interviews hold with representatives of the ministries, to prepare a pilot project and the review of the regulatory framework of Peru.

The identified process in each ministry is described, and its consistency with good RIA practices of the OECD countries is evaluated.

Process to issue regulations in the Ministry of Economy and Finance

Figure 5.1 shows the process to issue regulations identified in the Ministry of Economy and Finance (MEF).

Figure 5.1. Process to issue regulations in the MEF

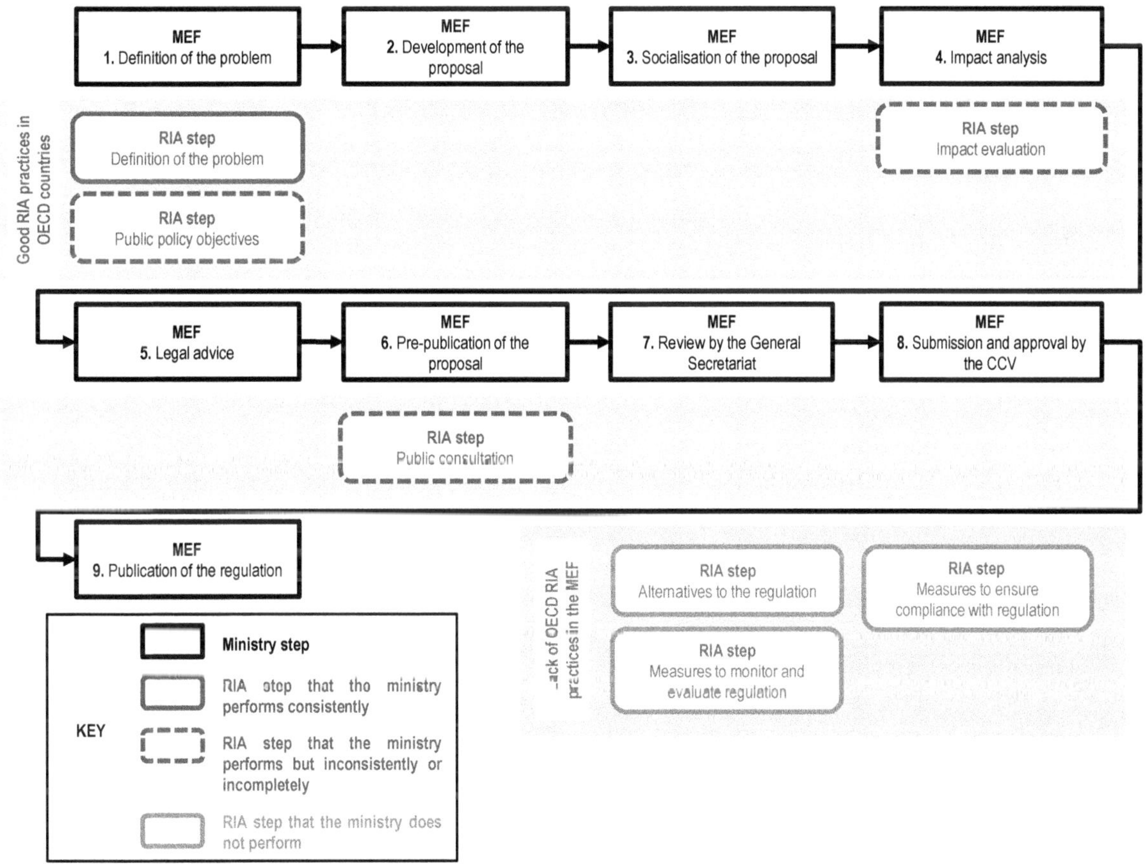

1. Definition of the problem

The first in the MEF is the definition of the problem. There is not a systematised process in the MEF to identify the problem, such as a checklist of questions or criteria. Nevertheless, enough evidence was found in the cases reviewed (see Chapter 2) to conclude that the definition of the problem is consistent with the RIA practices.

In this stage, there are efforts in the MEF to define public policy objectives. In general, the objectives to be achieved are described in the explanatory statement of the regulations. There are still, however, important areas of opportunity to provide a clear definition of the public policy objective, especially in the case of high-impact regulations, where the objectives to be reached should be defined in terms of parameters.

2. Development of the proposal

After the identification of the problem, the MEF draws up the regulatory proposal in the offices with authority to perform this task.

3. Socialisation of the proposal

Once the proposal is prepared, it is subject to a socialisation stage, where other directorates of the MEF or agencies with shared tasks or relation to the subject matter examined make their comments on the proposal. The socialisation of the proposal is an ad hoc process and the comments received are not available to the public.

4. Impact analysis

After socialising the proposal with the areas and public entities interested in the subject, the MEF carries out an impact analysis. Before January 2017, this analysis was occasionally and unsystematically and, unless it was a multisector regulation and, consequently, reviewed by the CCV, there was no monitoring of its compliance. Even if the regulatory proposal was submitted to the CCV, there was not always an impact analysis. As of January 2017, the MEF, the MINJUSDH and the PCM created a committee – as a pilot programme – to review the impact analysis of regulatory proposals. This committee advice the bodies issuing regulation on how to perform the analysis, on a case-by-case basis. However, there are no formal guidelines for its operation yet (see Chapter 6).

The impact analysis can be quantitative or qualitative, as applicable. On very few occasions, however, the MEF does a quantitative impact analysis. Although it carries out a qualitative one more frequently, it is still not performed in a systematic way.

This area of opportunity is even more important for the MEF, since it is in the finance division where the availability of data is wider and, consequently, conditions are more favorable to perform a cost-benefit analysis.

5. Legal advice

The legal advice of regulatory proposals is a step prior to the pre-publication, and it is generally a responsibility of the legal office of the MEF. This advice has a twofold purpose: first, that the draft of the regulatory proposal meet the form requirements and, second, that there be no controversy with another legal instrument.

6. Pre-publication of the proposal

Once the legal office prepares and reviews the proposal, the MEF pre-publishes it in the Official Gazette *El Peruano*, and on its transparency website. This publication is mandatory due the Supreme Decree DS-001-2009-JUS on its Article 14, which states the obligation of publishing general regulatory proposals in the Official Gazette *El Peruano*, on the websites or in any other medium for a minimum period of thirty days.

The main opportunity area of the pre-publication of regulatory proposals lies in their legal basis, since it does not mentions an obligation regarding the handling of public comments. That is, the ministries are not obliged to publish the comments or to reply to them, and although the MEF does so occasionally, it is not a common practice.

7. Review by the General Secretariat

With the final version of the proposal, the General Secretariat of the MEF conducts a final review to analyse the consistency of the regulation with the general administration and with the ministry itself.

8. Submission and approval by the CCV

The CCV must analyse the regulation involving multiple sectors for its approval. The nature and tasks of the CCV are explained in Box 5.1.

Box 5.1. Participation of the CCV in the ex ante evaluation of regulations

The Vice-Ministerial Coordinating Council (CCV) is the body that analyses and approves multisectoral regulation.1 It is comprised by the deputy ministers of the central government and the Secretary General of the Presidency of the Council of Ministers, who chairs the meetings. The CCV has three main tasks.2

1. Express a well-founded opinion about the Law Projects, Legislative Decree Projects, Urgency Decree Projects, Supreme Decree Projects and Supreme Resolution Projects that either require the approving vote of the Council of Ministers or are related to multiple sectors.
2. Facilitate the generation of input and recommendations in response to reports on multisectoral themes that are of high national interest or that affect the general policy of the government,
3. Approve the CCV rules of procedure.

According to the Presidency of the Council of Ministers, the CCV holds a standardised procedure with the help of ICT tools for the process of reviewing regulation. The process starts on Monday when the Coordination Secretariat of the PCM organises a tentative agenda for the week's meeting. After receiving and integrating the proposals from the ministries, the Premier decides what is to be included in the agenda and it sends an invitation for the weekly voting meeting to be held on Thursday. Before the meeting, the 35 deputy ministers have until Wednesday to upload in the digital platform the observations, comments, and corresponding documentation. The possible range of status of the draft regulatory instruments after the assessment of the CCV is the following:

- Viable without observations;

- Viable with observations;
- Not viable, and
- Viable with comments.

The matters considered as comments are those regarding grammatical and formatting aspects such as commas, numerals, etc. The observations, on the other hand, contain a discussion about the substance of the regulatory projects. When comments arise, the meeting discusses them on Thursday. In contrast, the observations have to be thoroughly discussed and they often cause the regulation to stall in the CCV. The voting is generally delivered physically during the meetings, although the deputy Ministries who are not able to attend the meetings can use the CCV's digital platform.

1. 1.3. About the Ministerial Resolution N° 251-2013-PCM: General Rules of the Vice-Ministerial Coordination Council.
2. Art. 4. Ibid.

Source: (OECD, 2016[2]), *Regulatory Policy in Peru: Assembling the Framework for Regulatory Quality*, OECD Reviews of Regulatory Reform, Paris, http://dx.doi.org/10.1787/9789264260054-en.

9. Publication of the regulation

Once the CCV approval is available, if it refers to multisectoral regulation or, in the rest of the cases, when the MEF sends directly the regulation, the proposal is published in the Official Gazette *El Peruano*. In the case of Ministerial Resolutions, for law-level regulation, they would have to follow their process for sending it to the Congress.

Lack of RIA practices

In the process to prepare the regulation, there was no evidence that the MEF performs an analysis of the necessary measures to ensure compliance with regulations, nor of the measures taken for monitoring and evaluating the regulation.

Likewise, before implementing the pilot committee for reviewing the impact analysis of regulatory proposals introduced in January 2017, no evidence was found that in the preparation process the MEF perform an analysis of alternatives to the regulation.

Process to issue regulations in the Ministry of Production

Figure 5.2 shows the identified process to issue regulations in the Ministry of Production (PRODUCE).

1. Definition of the problem

The first step identified in PRODUCE is the definition of the problem. PRODUCE employs thematic working groups with the relevant actors to discuss recurrently the problems that affect the sector. This is consistent with the "early consultation" practice, that can help to define the nature and scale of the problems (see Chapters 7 and 8). Depending on the subject in question, Produce invited to participate representatives of the industry, other ministries and, even, occasionally, officials from the municipalities.

In this stage, there are efforts in PRODUCE to define public policy objectives. In general, the objectives to be achieved are described in the explanatory statement of the regulations. There are still, however, important areas of opportunity to provide a clear definition of the public policy objective.

Figure 5.2. Process to issue regulations in PRODUCE

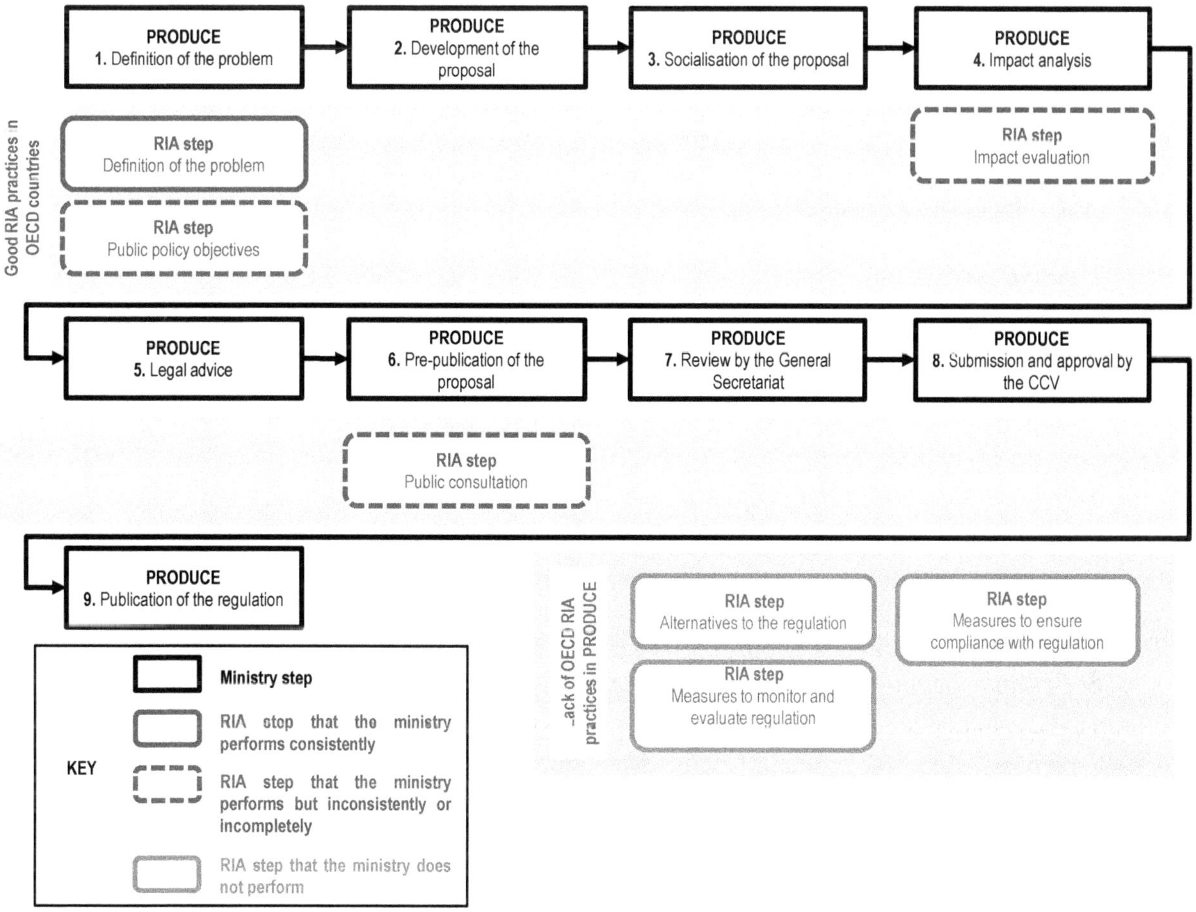

2. Development of the proposal

After the identification of the problem, PRODUCE draws up the regulatory proposal in the relevant offices with authority to issue regulations.

3. Socialisation of the proposal

Once the proposal is prepared, PRODUCE socialises it with other areas of the same ministry or agencies with shared tasks or relation to the subject matter examined, so that they make comments on the proposal. The socialisation of the proposal is an *ad hoc* process and the comments received are not available to the public.

4. Impact analysis

After socialising the proposal with the areas and public entities interested in the subject, PRODUCE carries out an impact analysis. Before January 2017, PRODUCE did this analysis occasionally and unsystematically, there was no monitoring of its compliance unless it was a multisectoral regulation and the CCV had to review it; moreover, there was not always an impact analysis. It is also performed a proportionality analysis, but it depends on the size of the alterations to the industry.

As of January 2017, the MEF, the MINJUSDH and the PCM created a committee – as a pilot programme – to review the impact analysis of regulatory proposal. This committee advises the regulation-issuing bodies on how to perform it, on a case-by-case basis, although there are no formal guidelines.

On very few occasions, PRODUCE does a quantitative impact analysis; although it carries out a qualitative one, it is not performed in a systematic way. There is a Directorate of Economic Studies subordinated to the General Secretariat that could do the impact analyses of regulations in a systematic way.

5. Legal advice

The legal advice of the regulatory proposals is a step prior to the pre-publication, and it is generally a responsibility of the legal office of PRODUCE. This advice has a twofold purpose: first, that the draft of the regulatory proposal meets the form requirements and, second, that there is no controversy with another legal instrument.

6. Pre-publication of the proposal

Once the proposal has been prepared and reviewed by the legal office, it sends it to the General Secretariat for its pre-publication in the Official Gazette *El Peruano* and on its transparency website, based on the Supreme Decree DS-001-2009-JUS. The article 14 of it states the obligation of publishing general regulatory proposals in the Official Gazette *El Peruano*, on the websites or in any other medium, for a minimum period of thirty days.

The main area of opportunity of the pre-publication of regulatory proposals lies in their legal basis, since the Supreme Decree does not mention an obligation on the handling of public comments. As a result, the ministries are not obliged to publish the comments or to reply to them; although PRODUCE does so occasionally, it is not a common practice.

7. Review by the General Secretariat

With the final version of the proposal, the General Secretariat of PRODUCE conducts a final review to analyse the consistency of the regulation with the general administration and with the ministry itself.

8. Submission and approval by the CCV

If the regulation involves multiple sectors, the relevant vice-ministerial office has to send it to the CCV for analysis and its approval.

9. Publication of the regulation

Once the CCV approves it, if it is a multisectoral regulation or PRODUCE sends the regulation directly, the proposal is published in *El Peruano*. In the case of Ministerial Resolutions, for law-level regulation, it has to follow the process for sending it to the Congress..

Lack of RIA practices

In the process to prepare the regulation, there is no evidence that PRODUCE performs an analysis of the necessary measures to ensure compliance with regulations, nor of the measures taken for monitoring and evaluating the regulation. Regarding an oversight function, the responsibility is split: on one side, the OEFA supervises the environmental tasks, while in others it depends on the sector, for instance, fisheries; consequently, there is not a division in charge of the sanctioning procedures and oversight on a crosscutting basis.

Likewise, before implementing the pilot committee to review the impact analysis of regulatory proposals introduced in January 2017, there is no evidence that PRODUCE performs an analysis of alternatives to the regulation in the process to prepare regulations.

Process to issue regulations in the Ministry of Environment

Figure 5.3 shows the process to issue regulations identified in the Ministry of Environment (MINAM).

Figure 5.3. Process to issue regulations in the MINAM

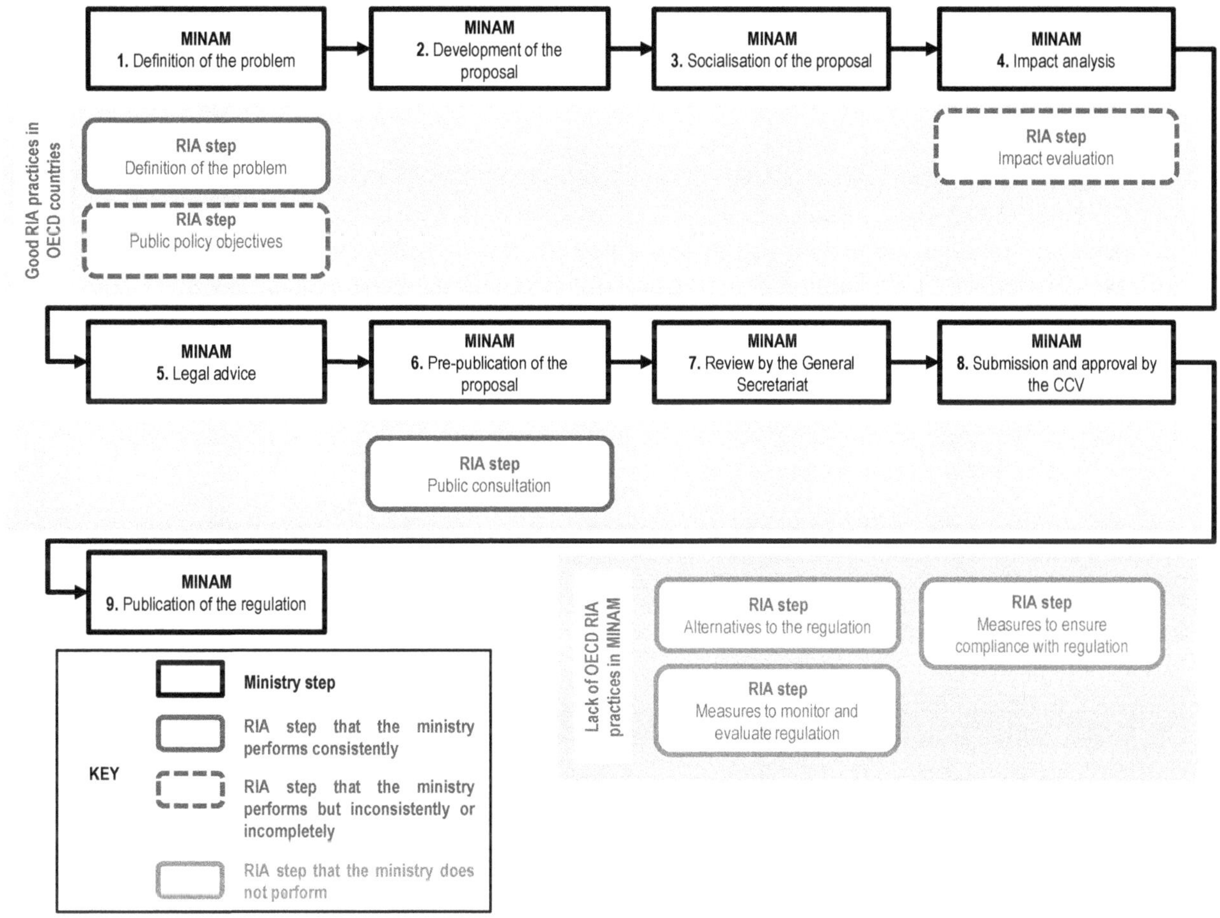

1. Definition of the problem

The first step identified in the MINAM is the definition of the problem. The MINAM usually holds informal meetings with representatives from the regulated sectors to collect information and define better the problem. They do this through forums, workshops, and working groups. They also employ international environmental programs to define the existence of a problem in which they must step in. This activity is consistent with the "early consultation" practice, that can help to define the nature and scale of the problems (see Chapters 7 and 8).

In this stage, there are efforts in the MINAM to define public policy objectives. In general, the objectives to be achieved are described in the explanatory statement of the regulations. Nevertheless, there are still important areas of opportunity to provide a clear definition of the public policy objective, for political or media conditions in some cases determine the definition of the problem, rather than by facts based on evidence.

2. Development of the proposal

After the identification of the problem, the MINAM draws up the regulatory proposal in the competent division according to the subject matter.

3. Socialisation of the proposal

Once MINAM prepares the proposal, the Ministry socialises it with other areas of the same ministry or agencies with shared tasks or relation to the subject matter examined, so that they make comments on the proposal. As this is an *ad hoc* process, the comments received are not available to the public.

4. Impact analysis

After socialising the proposal with the areas and public entities interested in the subject, the MINAM carries out an impact analysis. As the MINAM lacks information, in few occasions this analysis is done in a quantitative way. It usually does it in a qualitative way, even sometimes it performs a comparison with international benchmarks. However, the impact analysis is not systematical.

As of January 2017, the MEF, the MINJUSDH and the PCM created a committee – as a pilot programme – to review the impact analysis of regulatory proposals. This committee advises the regulation-issuing bodies on how to perform it, on a case-by-case basis, although there are no formal guidelines.

One of the main limitations the MINAM reports is the lack of data to perform the assessments and the lack of capacity building workshops for staff. Chapter 7 recommends strategies for data collection and training.

Legal advice

Prior to the pre-publication, the proposal is sent to the legal advice unit of MINAM's legal office. This advice has a twofold purpose: first, that the draft meets the form requirements or legislative technique ones and, second, that there be no controversy with another instrument of the legal framework in force.

6. Pre-publication of the proposal

Once the proposal has been prepared and reviewed by the legal office, the MINAM continues with the pre-publication in the Official Gazette *El Peruano* and on its transparency website, based on the Supreme Decree DS-001-2009-JUS. The article 14 of it states the obligation of publishing general regulatory proposals in *El Peruano*, on the websites or in any other medium, for a minimum period of thirty days. Furthermore, the MINAM has the obligation to conduct an early consultation according to the regulatory framework of the sector.

The main area of opportunity of the pre-publication of regulatory proposals lies in their legal basis, since it does not mentions any obligation regarding the handling of public comments. That is, the ministries are not obliged to publish the comments or to reply to them.

Nevertheless, a practice that is considered appropriate – but only carried out by the MINAM – consists in preparing a matrix of comments for its publication and analysis after the pre-publication. The MINAM collects public comments and includes them in a matrix of comments. This matrix includes the responses from the MINAM to public comments.

Afterwards, the MINAM holds meetings with the groups that made comments in order to clarify and clear up doubts. The MINAM anew draws up the regulatory proposal with the information obtained from the meetings. As MINAM's consultation practice is more advanced and consistent with RIA practices in the OECD countries, this should be replicated in all ministries.

7. Review by the General Secretariat

With the final version of the proposal, the responsible area sends it to the General Secretariat of MINAM to check the legal compliance. That is, to analyse the consistency of regulation with the general public administration and with the ministry itself.

8. Submission and approval by the CCV

If the regulation involves multiple sectors, the Ministry has to send it to the CCV for analysis and its approval.

9. Publication of the regulation

Once the CCV approves it, if it is a multisectoral regulation or when the MINAM send the regulation directly, the proposal is published in the Official Gazette *El Peruano*. In the case of Ministerial Resolutions, for law-level regulation, it has to follow the process for sending it to the Congress.

Lack of RIA practices

In the process to prepare the regulation, the MINAM does not performs an analysis of the measures necessary to ensure compliance with regulations, nor of the measures taken for monitoring and evaluating the regulation.

Likewise, before implementing the pilot committee to review the impact analysis of regulatory proposals introduced in January 2017, in the process to prepare regulations the MINAM does not performs an analysis of alternatives to the regulation.

Process to issue regulations in the Ministry of Transport and Communications

Figure 5.4 shows the process to issue regulations identified in the Ministry of Transport and Communications (MTC)

1. Definition of the problem

The first step identified in the MTC is the definition of the problem. The experience of the MTC –in telecommunications –includes the co-ordination with the Supervisory Agency for Private Investment in Telecommunications (OSIPTEL) for the understanding of the regulatory problems. As to the transportation sector, based on the scale of the problem or the impact it might have on a certain industry, it could previously decide to meet for delineating and defining whether or not there is a problem that should be addressed.

In this stage, there are efforts in the MTC to define public policy objectives. In general, the objectives to be achieved are described in the explanatory statement of the regulations. There are still, however, important areas of opportunity to provide a clear definition of the public policy objective.

2. Development of the proposal

After the identification of the problem, it draws up the draft proposal according to the sector: telecommunications or transportation.

Figure 5.4. Process to issue regulations in the MTC

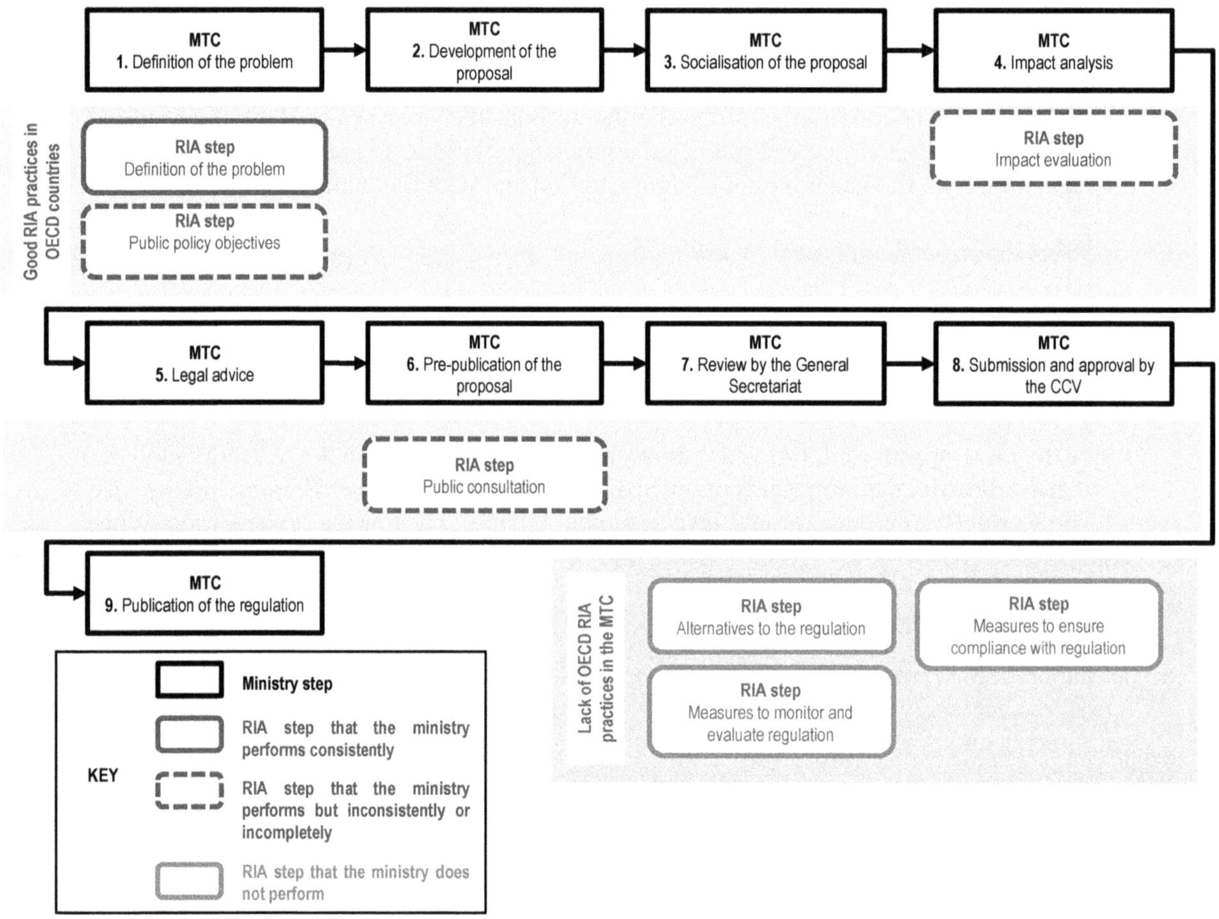

3. Socialisation of the proposal

Once the MTC prepares the project, it is subject to a socialisation stage, where other directorates of the Ministry or agencies as well as the regulated companies, make their comments on the proposal. As this is a non-standardised process, the comments received are not available to the public.

Impact analysis

After socialising the proposal with the areas and public entities interested in the subject, the MTC carries out an impact analysis. Before January 2017, MTC did this analysis occasionally and unsystematically, there was no monitoring of its compliance unless it was a multisectoral regulation and the CCV had to review it. Even when the Ministry submits the proposal to the CCV, there is not always an impact analysis.

As of January 2017, the MEF, the MINJUSDH and the PCM created a committee – as a pilot programme – to review the impact analysis of regulatory proposals. It advises the regulation-issuing bodies on how to perform it, on a case-by-case basis, although there are no formal guidelines.

On very few occasions, the MTC does a quantitative impact analysis. Although it carries out a qualitative one, it is not systematically.

One of the main limitations the MTC reports is the lack of data to perform the evaluations and the time needed to do so, and not so much the training of officials, since they have personnel with a high technical level who make international comparisons with other countries to remedy the shortcomings of data. Chapter 7 recommends strategies for data collection

5. Legal advice

Once the proposal is ready, it is sent to the MTC's legal office so that it verifies, on one hand, the requirements of legislative technique and, on the other, that it does not opposes another legal instrument.

6. Pre-publication of the proposal

Once the legal office draws up and reviews the proposal, the MTC pre-publicises it in the Official Gazette *El Peruano* and on its transparency website, based on the Supreme Decree DS-001-2009-JUS. Its Article 14 states the obligation of publishing general regulatory proposals in *El Peruano*, on the websites or in any other medium for a minimum period of thirty days.

The main area of opportunity of the pre-publication of regulatory proposals lies in their legal basis, since it does not mentions any obligation regarding the handling of public comments. That is, the ministries are not obliged to publish the comments or to reply to them; although the MTC does so occasionally.

7. Review by the General Secretariat

Once the final version of the proposal is available, the General Secretariat of the MTC conducts a final review to analyse the coherence of regulation with the regulatory framework in force of both the general administration and the ministry itself.

8. Submission and approval by the CCV

The CCV must analyse and approve if the proposal is a multisectoral regulation. The relevant vice-ministry has to send it to it.

9. Publication of the regulation

Once the CCV approves it, if it is a multisectoral regulation or, the MTC sends it directly, the proposal is published in the Official Gazette *El Peruano*. In the case of Ministerial Resolutions, for law-level regulation, the Ministry has to follow the process to send it to the Congress.

Lack of RIA practices

In the process to prepare the regulation, the MTC does not performs an analysis of the measures necessary to ensure compliance with regulations, nor of the measures taken for monitoring and evaluating the regulation.

Likewise, before implementing the pilot committee to review the impact analysis of regulatory proposals introduced in January 2017, in the process to prepare regulations the MTC does not perform an analysis of alternatives to the regulation.

Process to issue regulations in the Ministry of Housing, Construction and Sanitation

Figure 5.5 shows the process to issue regulations identified in the Ministry of Housing, Construction and Sanitation (VIVIENDA).

Figure 5.5. Process to issue regulations in VIVIENDA

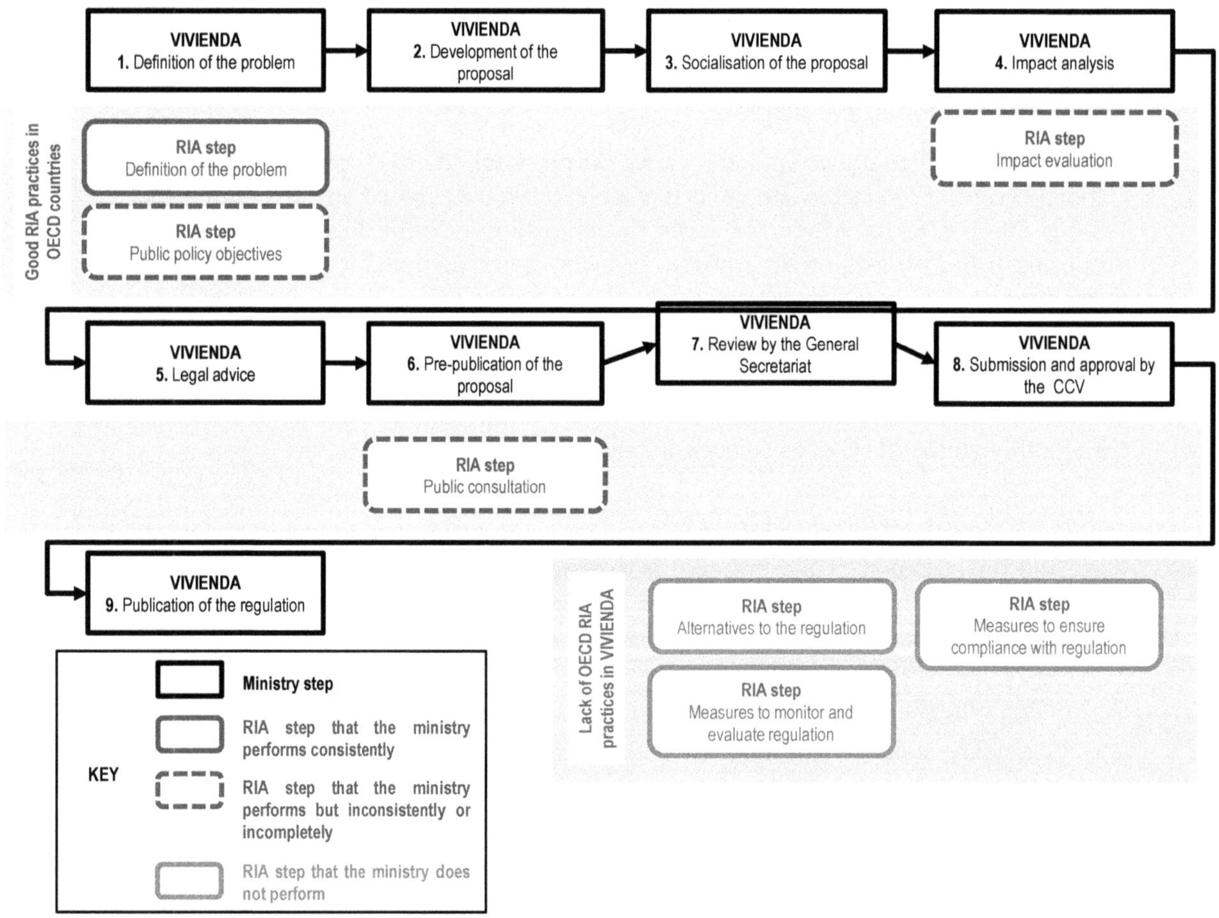

1. Definition of the problem

The first step identified in VIVIENDA is the definition of the problem. There is not a systematised process in VIVIENDA to identify the problem, such as a checklist of questions or criteria. Nevertheless, enough evidence was found in the cases reviewed (see Chapter 2) to conclude that the definition of the problem is consistent with the RIA practices.

There are efforts in VIVIENDA to define public policy objectives. In general, the objectives are described in the explanatory statement of the regulations. There are still, however, important areas of opportunity to provide a clear definition of the public policy objective.

2. Development of the proposal

After the identification of the problem, VIVIENDA draws up the regulatory proposal in the competent division according to the subject matter.

Socialisation of the proposal

Once VIVIENDA prepares the project, it is subject to a socialisation stage, where other directions or agencies make comments on the proposal. The socialisation of the proposal is a non-standardised process and the comments received are not available to the public. However, when the matters are responsibility of this ministry and they affect different levels of government – such as urban planning –, VIVIENDA must socialise the regulatory proposal with, for instance, municipalities. The latter promotes the regulatory co-ordination at subnational level.

4. Impact analysis

After socialising the proposal with the areas and public entities interested in the subject, VIVIENDA carries out an impact analysis. Before January 2017, MTC did this analysis occasionally and unsystematically, there was no monitoring of its compliance unless it was a multisectoral regulation and the CCV had to review it; moreover, there was not always an impact analysis.

As of January 2017, the MEF, the MINJUSDH and the PCM created a committee – as a pilot programme – to review the impact analysis of regulatory proposals. This committee advises the regulation-issuing bodies on how to perform it, on a case-by-case basis, although there are no formal guidelines.

On very few occasions, VIVIENDA does a quantitative impact analysis. Although it carries out a qualitative one, it is not performed systematically. Moreover, there is not a technical unit that is specifically in charge of conducting these analyses, but rather the same units that draw up the regulations are the ones that do so. Therefore, the level and thoroughness of that task depends on each of them.

5. Legal advice

Once the regulatory proposal is ready, it is sent to the legal advice office, which will verify it meets the requirements of form and legislative technique, and that it do not oppose any other previously existing regulation.

6. Pre-publication of the proposal

Once the legal office draws up and reviews the proposal, VIVIENDA continues with the pre-publication in the Official Gazette *El Peruano* and on its transparency website, based on the Supreme Decree DS-001-2009-JUS. Its Article 14 states the obligation of publishing general regulatory proposals in *El Peruano*, on the websites or in any other medium for a minimum period of thirty days.

The main area of opportunity of the pre-publication of regulatory proposals lies in their legal basis, since it does not mentions any obligation regarding the handling of public comments. That is, the ministries are not obliged to publish the comments or to reply to them, and although VIVIENDA does so occasionally, it is not a common practice.

7. Review by the General Secretariat

After the pre-publication of the proposal, the final version of the proposal is drawn up and the General Secretariat of VIVIENDA conducts a final review to analyse the coherence of regulation with the general administration and the ministry itself.

8. Submission and approval by the CCV

If it is a multisectoral regulatory proposal, the CCV must analyse it for its approval.

9. Publication of the regulation

If it refers to multisectoral regulation, once the CCV approves it, the proposal is published in the Official Gazette *El Peruano*. In the case of Ministerial Resolutions, for law-level regulation, the Ministry has to follow the process to send it to the Congress.

Lack of RIA practices

In the process to prepare the regulation, VIVIENDA does not performs an analysis of the measures necessary to ensure compliance with regulations, nor of the measures taken for monitoring and evaluating the regulation.

Likewise, before implementing the pilot committee to review the impact analysis of regulatory proposals introduced in January 2017, in the process to prepare regulations VIVIENDA does not performs an analysis of alternatives to the regulation.

General evaluation of the process to issue regulations in Peru

In general, the process for issuing regulations within the five selected ministries is virtually the same. The most important exception on the Ministry of Environment (MINAM), which performs a deeper consultation process that observes good RIA practices. While, in the other ministries, carrying out the process depends on the type of regulation and its relevance.

Lack of a standardised process with legal basis

The processes described before that focuses on the period 2014-16 are the ones the Ministries use to issue regulation. However, its use is a non-standardised practice, for there is not a specific instrument of regulatory policy that supports them – even though they exist some institutions and legal practices. In particular, in the process identified, only four steps have a legal basis:

- Impact analysis
- Pre-publication of the proposal
- Submission and approval by the CCV (in the case of multisectoral regulation)
- Publication of the regulation

It is evident that in this process there is no formalised oversight nor accountability regarding the way of issuance of the regulation, at least from a comprehensive point of view. As of January 2017, the government set up a pilot programme to perform an impact analysis, but it does not have yet a legal basis nor is mandatory.

The practice of any process to promote quality in regulation is at risk for this lack of formality, as it is very easy to eliminate these practices or ignore the established criteria, regardless of their technical strength.

The lack of formality also threatens the standardisation and transversality of the regulatory policy. Without the legal obligation of implementing the RIA and no supervisory body that enforces it, the purpose of promoting quality in regulation is limited. In fact, the incentives to officials so they observe the RIA discipline are not the same under specific legal obligations than without them.

The lack of formality increases the risk of regulatory capture because there are no institutionalised mechanisms that confront the validity, relevance, and necessity of the regulation. The lack of accountability in a controlled and transparent process of *ex ante* evaluation of the regulations creates a greater risk that actors have a negative influence on the regulation. Promoting regulations (via public consultation processes) is a mechanism of public action to be accountable and improve the regulatory proposal. However, if this process is not conducted under specific criteria, there is a greater risk of negative influence.[3]

On the other hand, in 2017 the process of elaboration and evaluation of the RQA began to work. Its objective is to identify, eliminate and/or simplify administrative procedures that are unnecessary, inefficient, unjustified, disproportionate, redundant or not adequate to the applicable regulatory framework. The RQA also aims to identify and reduce the administrative burdens of administrative procedures (see Chapter 4 for a more detailed description of the RQA).

In this process, Executive Branch entities seeking to issue or modify regulations and containing administrative procedures must prepare the RQA and submit it to the CCR chaired by PCM. The RQA must contain sufficient elements to enable the CCR to evaluate the legality, necessity, effectiveness, and proportionality of the administrative procedure (see Box 5.2 for more detail). The CCR may issue a binding report requesting modifications, validating administrative processes, or ordering their elimination if they are not validated.

The presentation and evaluation of the RQA is a stage prior to the publication of the regulation. The RQA introduces an element of discipline in the drafting of regulations in Peru, which contributes to the creation of a RIA system.

Box 5.2. RQA evaluation criteria

According to the Manual for the Application of Regulatory Quality Analysis, the public entities of the executive branch of Peru (EPPE) must analyse the principles of legality, necessity, effectiveness and proportionality of administrative procedures (AP) in order to perform the RQA:

Legality

- Determine the nature of the AP in order to categorise whether it produces legal effects on the interests, obligations or rights of those administered.
- Identify the competence of EPPE, to determine whether the competence is exclusive or shared with other levels of government.
- Identify or establish the legal basis of the AP and its requirements.

Necessity

- Identify the problem that the regulation linked to the AP intends to solve and the scope in which this problem occurs, if it is at the national, regional and/or local level.
- Determine AP's specific objective and the contribution it will bring on solving the problem. The specific objective must be achievable, relevant and measurable over time.
- Identify what the possible risks would be if the AP is removed or the new procedure proposal is not approved.
- Analyse whether there is an alternative that replaces the AP.

Effectiveness

- Analyse that each one of the requirements demanded contribute effectively to reach the object of the AP.
- To detect the requirements that are unnecessary or unjustified to the objective of the AP, for its later elimination.

Proportionality

- Analyse that each one of the requirements demanded contribute effectively to reach the object of the AP.
- Detect the requirements that are unnecessary or unjustified to the objective of the AP, for its later elimination.

In addition, EPPE must estimate the monetary and time costs of each of the requirements of the AP, so that the application used to deliver the RQA produces an estimate of the administrative burden of the AP.

Source: Ministerial Resolution No. 196-2017-PCM approving the Manual for the Application of Regulatory Quality Analysis (RM. 196 2017-PCM).

Definition of the problem and public policy objectives

According to the evidence showed of the period 2014-16, in Peru is recognised that on the issuance of regulation it is reflected the government's intention to solve a problem that has previously been identified. However, it is not common to set explicitly the public policy objective when addressing the identified problem.

It will be necessary to determine whether with the introduction of the RQA, the definition of the problem and of the public policy objectives in the regulatory issuing process is more effective. As indicated in Box 5.1, the analysis of the principles of necessity, effectiveness and proportionality can contribute to it.

Alternatives to the regulation and impact analysis

According to the evidence showed of the period 2014-16, in Peru there are initial efforts to carry out an impact evaluation of regulations, but much remains to be done to systematise this practice and raise the quality of the exercise.

The bylaw of the Congress lays down the obligation to perform cost-benefit analyses in draft bills. This bylaw indicates, "bills must include an explanatory statement detailing its rationale, the effect of the life of the regulation proposed on national legislation, including a cost-benefit analysis of the future legal rule." In practice, however, it is only included an analysis of the possible direct costs or of budgetary burdens that could be incurred by the State to carry out the proposal. It are mentioned neither the costs for the industry nor for the consumers.

Apart from the legal obligations of conducting an appropriate impact analysis, ministries face obstacles to carry it out. One of the most important problems to conduct those analyses is the availability of information or, if applicable, the lack of a methodology to obtain or produce it.

The impact evaluation should be prepared for all the identified alternatives to the regulation. Doing so would ensure that the regulation chosen be the most appropriate by producing the greatest benefit to society. In Peru, it is not necessary to carry out systematically an identification of alternatives.

With the introduction of the RQA as of 2017, it is expected that with the analysis of the principles of necessity, effectiveness, and proportionality, government entities would identify alternatives to regulation more effectively. In addition, since entities are required to calculate the costs of requirements, this can contribute to the preparation of a comprehensive cost-benefit analysis.

Notwithstanding the advantages that the RQA provides compared to the situation prevailing prior to its introduction, the RQA does not include requesting a cost-benefit analysis of the regulations that are intended to be issued or modified. In a RIA system the cost-benefit analysis, even qualitatively, is intended to contrast the benefits of the regulation as a whole against the costs that would be generated by its adoption.

Compliance with regulation

When a regulation is issued, it is necessary that civil servants identify in advance the mechanisms that are to be established, as well as the resources needed to ensure that the provisions stated therein will be observed. These could include oversight mechanisms, fines or other types of incentives. Although in Peru for the 2014-16 period some cases consider this type of mechanisms when issuing regulations, it is not a systematised practice.

Monitoring and evaluation

On the period 2014-16, Peru did not previously establishes indicators to measure the level of accomplishment of the public policy objectives intended to be reached, nor of the mechanisms to evaluate on an *ex post* basis if those objectives were achieved.

Public consultation

The public consultation of regulatory proposals is a key element that is constantly used to improve or narrow down the definition of the problem, obtain relevant information, identify stakeholders, and smooth out the process of adopting the new regulation by the actors involved. Currently, public consultation in Peru is called pre-consultation; and it is only used intermittently.

On the period 2014-16, the activities carried out by the MINAM after socialising the proposal stand out, namely, the creation of a matrix of comments, meetings with the commentators, and redeveloping the regulatory proposal. These activities should be systematically implemented in all the institutions from the central government of Peru. As well as the practice established in VIVIENDA of consulting the draft proposal among the different levels of government.

With respect to the RQA that became operational in 2017, its development and evaluation process does not include provisions to address the sections of regulatory compliance, monitoring and evaluation, and public consultation, which should be part of a RIA system.

Chapter 7 includes recommendations for adopting each of the essential stages of the RIA system in the process to issue regulations in Peru.

Notes

[1] Legislative Decree 1310 introduced the ACR evaluation procedure. It was published on December 30, 2016, and its provisions entered into force the following day.

[2] The description and analysis included in this chapter refer to the practices performed before the beginning of the RIA pilot program, introduced in January 2017. In any case, the conclusions of this chapter are important to reform that pilot programme.

[3] Peru's Energy and Mining Investment Supervisory Agency (OSINERGMIN) and Peru's Public Transport Infrastructure Investment Supervisory Agency (OSITRAN) have taken action to implement RIA. Both OSINERGMIIN and OSITRAN have published manuals for the development of RIA and are already using them in practice.

References

OECD (2016), *Regulatory Policy in Peru: Assembling the Framework for Regulatory Quality*, OECD Reviews of Regulatory Reform, OECD Publishing, Paris, https://dx.doi.org/10.1787/9789264260054-en. [2]

OECD (2012), *Recommendation of the Council on Regulatory Policy and Governance*, OECD Publishing, Paris, https://dx.doi.org/10.1787/9789264209022-en. [1]

Chapter 6. Evaluation of the building blocks of a RIA system in Peru

This chapter includes an evaluation of the level of adoption of each of the building blocks to introduce, design the necessary framework and prepare the implementation of the RIA in Peru. The OECD report on Building an Institutional Framework for Regulatory Impact Analysis (RIA), Guidance for Policy Makers *is used as a guide for such evaluation.*

Introduction

The OECD report *Building* an *Institutional Framework* for *Regulatory Impact Analysis (RIA)*, *Guidance* for *Policy Makers* (OECD, 2008[1]) identifies the subjects that must be addressed by an analyst to create the guiding framework for regulatory impact assessment (RIA). According to the report, regulators involved in regulatory-management matters and public policies should consider if there are some pre-existing conditions and to what extent current institutions can provide a good framework to implement the RIA, before venturing into the design and implementation of the RIA. The framework offered by the OCDE in this report highlights the questions that must be considered and the benefits of this tool to help professionals better understand the elements needed for a RIA system.

Figure 6.1 shows a summary of the building blocks needed to implement a RIA system, which also should be considered and evaluated by the analysts in charge of the regulatory policy. This chapter includes an analysis of the level of adoption of those building blocks in Peru, carried out by the OCED. The quotations of the next section explain the importance of each building block, and they are immediately followed by their corresponding assessment for Peru.

Evaluation

Introduction of the RIA

Before designing and implementing the RIA system in Peru, a series of elements that will effectively contribute to adopt and implement RIA for increasing the quality in the design of the regulation should be considered. These building blocks are described below:

1. Political commitment

   One of the essential factors for the adoption of the RIA is to have political support from the highest level, as this allows its implementation to be widely accepted as a new tool to create regulations; even by the agencies issuing them, who must modify their current methodologies y conduct these impact assessments while developing any new regulation.

Over the last years, the Peruvian government implemented a series of measures aimed to improve the quality of regulations through different high-level agencies. On the one hand, the PCM is responsible for the administrative simplification and the promotion of regulator quality, in which the RQA is a pivotal element. The MEF conducts an economic analysis of regulations, which has the objective of guaranteeing the coherence between the sectorial and the economic policies of the government. The MINJUSDH issued a manual on legislative technique to prepare regulatory proposals and, in certain cases, it also analyses the consistency of regulation with the legal framework in force; the CCV reviews and discusses multisectoral regulatory proposals. The National Institute for the Defense of Free Competition and Protection of Intellectual Property (INDECOPI), which reviews the existence of bureaucratic barriers. In addition to this, each ministry and government agency frequently have legal divisions who often perform a legal analysis of the regulatory proposals prepared by each regulator and, in some cases, they even have experts in economics, who conduct impact analyses of the regulatory proposals.

Figure 6.1. Building blocks necessary to implement a RIA system

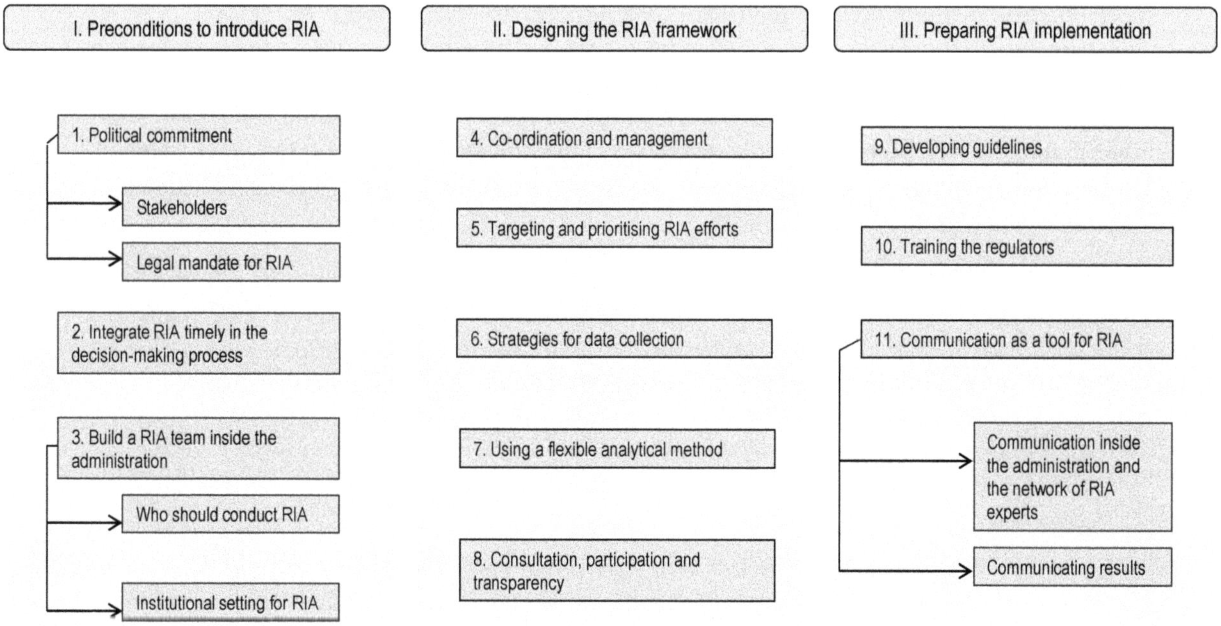

Source: (OECD, 2008[1]), *Building an Institutional Framework for Regulatory Impact Analysis (RIA): Guidance for Policy Maker*, OECD Publishing, Paris, http://dx.doi.org/10.1787/9789264050013-en.

However, within the public administration there are no cross-cutting instructions for the adoption of an *ex ante* evaluation system that acts as an analysis tool to assess the impact and regulatory quality, with the exception of the RQA. Although Legislative Decree N° 1310, its Bylaw and the Manual for the application of the Regulatory Quality Analysis are an unprecedented step for an *ex ante* evaluation of the regulation, it cannot be considered as a RIA system yet. These instruments establish a system of *ex ante* evaluation of regulatory proposals that focuses on the performance of an analysis of the formalities included in the proposal in question. Its objective is to evaluate the administrative procedures following the principles of legality, need and proportionality. Specifically, in the process of need these elements are evaluated i) identification of the public problem that the regulation seeks to solve; ii) the objective of the administrative procedure and if it exists a causal relation with the public problem; iii) analysis of different alternatives to the procedure and the risk in case its evaluation is produced. An element that could be added to the RQA is the evaluation of administrative procedures based on a comparison of potential costs and benefits. This, the RQA is a vital element for the *ex ante* evaluation of regulations in Peru, but it still requires further development to be considered a RIA system. However, the implementation of the Regulatory Quality Analysis underlines the fact that in Peru there is a political commitment for the *ex ante* evaluation of regulation, and that it could be used to introduced the RIA system, following the recommendations described in the next chapters.

In addition to the Regulatory Quality Analysis process that is a responsibility of the PCM, as of January 2017 a pilot committee, which was integrated by the PCM, MEF and MINJUSDH, was created to introduce the RIA for all draft regulations, as a pilot programme.

Finally, with the publication of the *Legislative Decree N° 1448 that modifies Article 2 of the Legislative Decree N° 1310, Legislative Decree that approves the additional administrative simplification measures and perfects the institutional framework and the instruments that rule the process of improvement of regulatory quality*, the bases for the implementation of a transversal and integral regulatory policy are established. In the Legislative Decree, RIA is defined as a tool for regulatory quality and mandates the PCM, MEF and MINJUSDH to emit a decree for the implementation of this tool. This is additional evidence that there is a political commitment in Peru for the formal and systematic adoption of a RIA system.

a. Stakeholders

Besides the political support, it is necessary that groups get involved both inside and outside of the public administration, that they acknowledge and assess the positive and negative conditions in the adoption of the RIA, and that also contribute to disseminate the use of this tool in the decision-making process. These groups can be integrated by public or private institutions, where the counseling offices of the presidency or the prime minister, the different ministries, parliaments, business and consumer associations, and academics participate.

Pursuant to Article 14 of the *Bylaw that lays down rules on advertising, publication of regulatory proposals, and dissemination of General Legal Rules*, public entities are obliged to publish in the Official Gazette *El Peruano* the general regulatory proposals that fall within their purview, this must be done at least 30 days before the scheduled date for their entry into force, as well as the deadline to receive comments. The above suggests that Peru has a formal mechanism to allow the participation of stakeholders in regulatory proposals. Nevertheless, this is done once the proposal has already been designed and not in advance. However, some ministries —such as MINAM and PRODUCE— have mechanisms for the participation of stakeholders before the regulatory proposal is prepared, for instance, advisory panels or workshops. Whereas, in others, performing this consultation depends on the regulation and the affected sector.

Furthermore, once the pre-publication of the regulatory proposal has been carried out and the comments are received, there is no formal obligation of responding to comments, although – in practice – it may be done.

b. Legal mandate for RIA

It is necessary that the government expresses its commitment to the use of RIA through a high-level regulatory instrument, that lays down clearly the standards and quality principles of the regulatory policy. To this end, different regulatory instruments have been employed in OECD countries, including laws, decrees, presidential decrees, guidelines *or resolutions of prime ministers or government resolutions, among others. Even, another way of expressing the political commitment for the use of this tool can be done by having the RIA instrument directly signed by a minister or a deputy minister.*

Currently, Peru has several normative instruments that influence the quality of the issuance of regulations. First of all, the Law of General Administrative Procedure, which lays down that regulation must observe the principles of rationality and proportionality. There is also the *Guide on Legislative Technique for the Development of Regulatory Proposals from the Entities of the Executive Branch*, which takes as reference the Law N° 26889, *Framework Law for Legislative Production and Systematization, which governs the guidelines for the preparation, titling and publishing of laws*, and its Bylaw, approved by Supreme Decree

N° 008-2006-JUS. These instruments, however, are directed to the writing up and structure that must be followed to prepare regulatory proposals, but not to the quality of the regulation; and if this is really necessary and produces greater benefits than costs to society. Likewise, as part of their processes to issue regulations and according to their internal rules, the legal office of each ministry examines and assesses the legal consistency of the regulatory instruments intended to be issued, in order to avoid duplication or conflict with the existing regulation. In the same way, part of the tasks of the MEF includes to carry out an economic analysis of the regulation; while the MINJUSDH reviews that the regulatory proposal does not oppose the Constitution nor federal laws, but this is only for the proposals that have been submitted before the Council of Ministers and the CCV. Moreover, on December 30, 2016, the Legislative Decree *N° 1310 approving additional administrative simplification measures* was issued; its Article 2 lays down that the entities of the Executive Branch must conduct a Regulatory Quality Analysis, but this is limited solely to rules that establish administrative procedures.

Finally, the Legislative Decree N° 1448 published on September 16, 2018 defines the regulatory quality policy in Peru, establishes the RIA as tool for regulatory quality and mandates the PCM, MEF and MINJUSDH to emit a decree for the implementation of RIA.

2. Integrate RIA timely in the decision-making process

As the regulatory impact assessment is a policy tool that helps to make decisions, it is necessary to integrate it into the effective policy-making process. RIA provides an assessment of regulatory alternatives and that is why it is crucial to integrate it at an early stage of the policy-making process, this will provide an initial phase of exchange and communication of the potential effects of legislation once it is passed.

So far, Peru has not formally nor systematically adopted all the stages that are an essential part of a RIA system as a tool within the policy-making process, with the exception of the contributions that the RQA makes to the definition of the problem, the public policy objective, identification of alternatives and some costs (see Chapter 5). It is necessary to integrate this impact analysis from an early stage of the policy-making process, so that it contributes efficiently to make decisions and achieve its objectives; otherwise, the RIA can become a tool to justify political decisions or, even, a barrier to issue regulation.

3. Build a RIA team inside the administration

The success of implementing the RIA also depends on the way a RIA team can be made up and strengthened inside the administration, which must be familiar with the current institutional setting. The consolidation of this team will be aimed at integrating this tool into the policy-making process.

There are several groups, within the public administration, whose powers have a bearing on the analysis of regulations; on one side, the MEF, which is responsible for carrying out an economic analysis and a cost-benefit analysis; on the other, the MINJUSDH, which conducts an analysis of the constitutionality and legality, as well as of the legal quality; and the PCM, which assesses whether the proposal is compatible with the organisation and operation of government and if it requires a RQA. These agencies act in an independent capacity and, in most cases, at the request of the entity sponsoring the regulatory proposal; they act collegially through the CCV, but only for multisectoral proposals or those that require the approval vote of the Council of Ministers. Furthermore, the Multisectoral Commission of Regulatory Quality (CCR), subordinated to the PCM, evaluates the Regulatory Quality Analysis of draft regulations. Lastly, the PCM, MEF and MINJUSDH participate in the pilot programme of RIA. Nevertheless, there is not a permanent team in charge of formally reviewing the quality of the regulatory proposals with a RIA[1] approach. On the contrary, there is a variety of actions and initiatives that still need to be articulated under a whole-of-government regulatory policy, although the process for the preparation and evaluation of the RQA is a step in this direction.

That is why an oversight body must be created with the explicit mandate of supervising the development process of new regulations, ensuring the quality of RIAs and regulatory proposals or, where appropriate, entrusting that responsibility to an entity within the central government, vested with extensive powers to direct the work of implementing the regulatory impact assessment in Peru.

a. Who should conduct RIA

Considering that several government agencies are the ones empowered to draft regulations, the RIA should be implemented within them; and since this tool requires multiple capacities, it is necessary to create cross-functional technical teams that contribute to draft the RIA with a comprehensive perspective, and have political, legal, economic and communication expertise.

Although each regulatory body within the public administration has several groups of their own able to carry out legal, economic or impact analyses, among others, these are not yet conducted in an articulated way and, in many cases, they only respond to the human resources available.

b. Institutional setting for RIA

There is not a unique institutional model for the systematic use of RIA, since among OECD countries there is a great variety of institutions sharing different responsibilities and working following different methodologies. Nevertheless, in general, it can be considered as a specialised department or group of experts in each line ministry and regulatory institution who undertake the RIA work. In order to ensure co-ordination among these bodies and to give coherence to the regulatory systems, there are two institutional set-ups:

- *Centralised institutional frameworks rely on an oversight body for regulatory reform, located at the center of government. In this case, its powers are supported by the highest political level (president, governor, prime minister, etc.) or by a budgetary decision-making institution (Ministry of Economy and Finance).*
- *Decentralised institutional frameworks do not rely on a specific oversight body, and the co-ordination among regulators is essential to obtain policy objectives. Responsibilities are normally shared by different regulatory institutions and line ministries, which use extended consultations mechanisms to reach agreements and consensus.*

Based on OECD experience, choosing either of the institutional frameworks for RIA often depends on the political support available, the original institutional framework, the political and public administration culture, the resources at hand and, more particularly, the existence of any general programme focused on regulatory governance and reform.

As noted, Peru has several agencies partially responsible for the quality of regulation with a RIA approach, but it does not yet have a supervisory body to oversee the development process of the new regulations that ensures the quality of RIA and the regulatory proposals.

Designing the RIA framework

Once preconditions have been created, the next step is to design the RIA process. The design phase involves examining each component of the proposed system for conducting RIA and determining its feasibility. This includes co-ordination mechanisms, targeting RIA efforts, improving data collection and using a flexible methodology for RIA. The components are described below:

4. Co-ordination and management

   A RIA system needs to be co-ordinated and carefully managed across the central ministries of government and other law-making institutions. Allocating responsibilities among regulators improves the "ownership" and integration by decision making agents that may generate opposition or badly articulated co-ordination mechanisms.

   In the ideal process, a preliminary RIA document undertaken by the institution initiating the proposal accompanies draft regulation or legislation; and an extended network of policy makers spread around the public administration working on RIA, for their own policy purposes specialised in different issues depending on their field of work, will contribute substantial content to the analysis of possible impacts.

   In order to consolidate co-ordination among all parties, some OECD countries have also established a central body with a leading role at a high political level, responsible for overseeing the RIA process and ensuring consistency.

   Moreover, a consistent methodology for RIA and its quality standards can be promoted with the provision of guidelines, ensuring that the process follows certain steps in a systematic way and that the final RIA document attains the desired quality level. In any case, increasing capacities inside the administration to conduct RIA is fundamental to make better use of this policy tool.

   The OECD experience shows that monitoring and oversight institutions offer quality control by providing basically three services to officials undertaking RIA:

   1) consultation and technical assistance in drafting RIA

   2) review of an individual RIA, and

   3) stocktaking of general compliance with RIA by law makers

   Although these institutions should be given the appropriate level of authority to ensure their effectiveness, adequate work is necessary to raise awareness among all parties, provided that the levels of authority vested allow for the participation in the usual public policy flows (i.e., right of veto), and prioritise the search for creative solutions in the face of systematic intervention in processes that involve abusing the powers conferred.

There are several agencies in charge, to a greater or lesser extent, of the regulatory quality in Peru with a RIA approach. In the case of multisectoral regulations, three agencies – that have shown great co-ordination – participate: PCM, MEF and MINJUSDH. However, this co-ordination is vague for regulations issued by a single ministry, except when participating in the Multisectoral Commission of Regulatory Quality. Currently, there is not a governing body for regulatory policy, but rather a group of agencies vested with certain powers that participate in the rule-making process.

5. Targeting and prioritising RIA efforts

Policy makers should target RIA towards regulatory proposals that have the largest impact on society and ensure that all such proposals be subject to close RIA scrutiny. At first, considering limited resources and aiming at familiarising civil servants and stakeholders with the new process, efforts should concentrate on the most challenging regulatory areas.

As RIA is an activity that requires an important degree of expertise and responsibility, it is essential to precisely define the regulation to which RIA is going to be applied. Ideally, it should be applied to high-impact regulations, where their benefits may be higher.

There is no practice in Peru of conducting a more exhaustive impact analysis for regulatory proposals of great importance, nor were criteria established to identify which regulatory proposals this type of assessments should be applied to.

6. Strategies for data collection

Data quality is an essential element for conducting a proper analysis. However, this is one of the most difficult parts of RIA because it can be time and resource consuming; consequently, it requires a systematic and functional approach. The usefulness of RIA depends on the quality of the data used to evaluate the impact of regulation. Hence, governments need to set up a functional framework for a quantitative analysis by developing precise and straightforward strategies and guidelines. This implies, as well, that policy makers need to gain certain skills, think in quantitative terms and get acquainted with the collection of the necessary data for each particular case.

Although a large amount of data is collected through the consultation process, there are numerous ways and sources to get it (in-house expertise of economists, lawyers and analysts; commission research and studies; dedicated RIA training, networking for RIA; international data and best practices; and so forth).

According to the information gathered in the different ministries, there are several data collecting strategies that contribute to the analysis of the draft proposal. Some ministries conduct early consultations with in-house stakeholders and external ones to the public administration. In other cases, the statistical information existing within the ministry itself is used or, even, national and international statistical information is checked, or desk research is also carried out (bibliographic sources, Internet, etc.); but there is not a homogeneous or defined method for a systematic data collection.

7. Using a flexible analytical method

Determining which method to apply is a central element of RIA design and performance. There are several methods used, such as cost-benefit analysis, cost-effectiveness or cost-output analysis, fiscal or budget analysis, socio-economic impact analysis, risk analysis, consequence analysis, compliance cost analysis and business impact tests.

At first, it is common to start with an assessment of costs and quantify the benefits later on. Nevertheless, the latter is a more complicated task since benefits are usually more difficult to measure.

Efforts should be scaled to the specific capacities of each country or region, considering the available resources to collect and analyse the required information. It is not about conducting complex technical analyses but about asking the right questions to the right people.

In nearly all countries, there are a number of instruments that may be used as pillars for the development of a RIA system, among which stand out the legal justifications (notes attached to the laws) or the budget and environmental impact assessments.

The same analytical process applies to the multisectoral regulations that must be examined by the CCV: an economic analysis performed by the MEF, a legislative technique analysis by the MINJUSDH, and an administrative simplification and regulatory quality analysis by the PCM. In the case of regulations issued by an entity, each of them performs different assessments, based on their economic and human resources available, as well as on the relevance of the regulation, plus the Regulatory Quality Analysis of the PCM. However, the legal analysis —that is done at the same time— examines the consistency with the regulatory framework in force. Moreover, some ministries perform a cost-benefit analysis, although in some cases they are more qualitative than quantitative or, in the case of the MTC, differential analyses are also carried out. Likewise, proportionality analyses are carried out but they are done intuitively, because there is not a standardised methodology.

8. Consultation, participation and transparency

RIA can only be legitimate and efficient if it is integrated into public consultation procedures. The systematic integration of stakeholders' views undoubtedly enhances the quality of this tool. Therefore, consulting these groups can furnish very important information on the feasibility of the proposals. Likewise, it also increases the likelihood compliance, as the ownership of the proposed regulation is shared with these stakeholders.

It is possible to increase the amount of data available for decision-making and reduce the risk of "data capture" by opening the process and involving all stakeholders.

Likewise, the RIA system can only add value if it increases transparency and participation in the regulatory process, and the only way to achieve so is by involving the public. In this sense, stakeholders should be incorporated from the early stages of the process, participating in the assessment of the need for regulation and in the design of the RIA document itself.

There is a procedure for the participation of stakeholders through the pre-publication of regulatory proposals, the *Bylaw that lays down rules on establishes provisions for the advertisement, publication of regulatory proposals and dissemination of general legal rules* lays down in its Article 14 that stakeholders should be allowed to make their comments on the regulatory proposals. However, there is no harmonised or formal procedure to respond to the comments received.

On one hand, each ministry has several types of consultation that are performed at different times of the development of the regulation and respond to different circumstances. For instance, the MTC conducts specific consultations on telecommunications with certain sector groups; whereas, in the case of transport, it carries them out based on the interests of the regulation. As to the MINAM, it has a specific regulation on transparency and citizen participation for environmental matters; and they consult both with technical groups and with the public at large. PRODUCE, on its part, also makes preliminary consultations through the delivery of workshops. The MEF makes the consultation calling through e-mail or official communication with the ministry related to the activity to be regulated and, to a lesser extent, with trade associations. Most of the time, the regulatory proposal is also posted on the website of each ministry.

In general, although a public consultation is carried out with the pre-publication of the draft proposal, it is done after the proposal has been defined. On the other, in most of the cases preliminary consultations are not formal.

Preparing the implementation of the RIA

The implementation phase of this new policy tool requires, besides training, to become familiar with it, particularly by those who draw up the regulatory proposals, because this new methodology involves a cultural change within the public administration. Therefore, it is important to take into account the following factors:

9. Developing guidelines

Aiming at facilitating capacity building processes on RIA, many countries' authorities have drafted clear, concise and accessible guidelines, where theory and practical methodology are explored and in which the use of this policy tool is explained. These documents tend to cover a wide range of issues, but usually they are understood as "living documents" that can be continuously improved as experiences and knowledge of RIA issues accumulate and new techniques or methodological changes are embraced.

It is essential to have a series of mandatory basic guidelines at the highest level (laws and regulation), and it is advisable to detail them in an operating manual and/or rely on a consulting firm that can advise on their application and interpretation.

In most OECD countries, central oversight bodies for regulatory reform are in charge of drafting and distributing these guidelines. If these institutions are not responsible for the training on RIA, strong co-ordination mechanisms should be arranged in a timely manner.

The legal instruments available in Peru, described in Chapter 4, do not include a manual nor specific guidelines to perform the RIA. The only instrument including a specific guide for an *ex ante* evaluation of regulations is the Manual for the application of the Regulatory Quality Analysis, but it focuses solely on the legislation that includes administrative procedures.

10. Training the regulators

Training and capacity building are the most important factors for the success of RIA implementation and systematisation. First, training and capacity building programmes should be established to familiarise officials with their obligations about RIA and the use of its guidelines. At a later stage, properly designed training programmes should be conducted to give regulators the skills needed to undertake high quality RIA as well as providing information on where to get advice with more complex cases. At this stage, it is necessary to thoroughly apply the methodologies for measuring impact and rely on the expertise of relevant practitioners.

This training, however, should not only be targeted to regulators, but should also include civil society and business associations to promote their participation and the addition of more value to public consultation or promote other public policies of their interest with the appropriate support.

Once RIA is introduced in the regulatory process, practical problems may occur more often than technical ones derived from misunderstanding or ignorance of theoretical aspects of RIA. This is why training and capacity building on RIA are of vital importance for its success.

As the use of RIA implies a change of culture in public administration, as already mentioned, it is important to establish training programs, first, to make it known in all government levels and, second, the usefulness and benefits of using this tool, as well as its scope to create public policy alternatives.

Knowledge about this tool has begun to be disseminated in the Peruvian government, workshops have even been delivered with the MEF and other ministries and public entities, including PCM, MINJUSDH, MTC, PRODUCE, MINAM, VIVIENDA, as well as the supervisory agencies (OSINERGMIN and OSITRAN). Nevertheless, it is important to create ongoing training programs that even consider the preparation of a RIA and its analysis.

11. RIA as a communication tool

There are mainly two aspects of communication that have a major impact on a RIA system. First, the communication within the public administration to ensure coherence and co-ordination, and second, the communication of results to all parties involved and interested that may be outside the administration.

Although some activities have been carried out to begin disseminating the use of RIA as the next tool of the public administration to draw up regulations, namely, training workshops, there are still no relevant plans or programs to make it known to all entities and at all levels, as well as to stakeholders. This is particularly important so as to RIA be an efficient tool and widely used by all regulators, as well as to convince stakeholders and even public at large of its usefulness as guarantee of regulatory quality.

a. Communication inside the administration and the network of RIA experts

RIA is a policy tool that should be used by officials working in different government agencies. To ensure co-ordination and coherence in their work, effective communication channels must be established. This communication should be established through a technical network of practitioners to bring the benefits of the exchange of information and share experiences. Furthermore, it is crucial that the activities of all regulators implementing RIA are co-ordinated in an adequate and systematic way to complement and increase communication among them.

According to several current procedures for drawing up regulations, there are some co-ordination processes among some government entities, for instance, to draw up multisectoral regulation, where the PCM, MEF and MINJUSDH participate in a co-ordinated manner. However, for the regulation issued by a single ministry, the co-ordination among several entities is not so formal and it is limited to transfer the draft proposal from one division to the next, so that each of them conducts the corresponding analysis.

b. Communicating results

A major impact of RIA lies in its capacity to show the different possible ways to proceed when putting forward a law proposal. RIA activities should be reviewed and the results communicated, in order to draw lessons from the whole process. This implies not only the release of RIAs along with draft regulatory texts as part of the consultation procedure, but also to record those cases in which the RIA system succeeded in weeding out inefficient regulatory proposals before enactment.

Communication is a key element of RIA and must be in alignment with the policy objectives of the regulation under analysis. The institutions responsible for RIA communication should be clear about who is affected by the analysed regulation, so communication can be well targeted to all stakeholders.

Lastly, bibliography should be provided in the annexes to the RIA so that interested users can find the background information employed to undertake the RIA.

In the current process of drawing up regulations, some ministries follow different steps to show to (in-house and external) stakeholders the results of the regulatory process. For example, MINAM and PRODUCE make preliminary consultations should a problem arise and they decide to step in as regulators to solve it; with this they determine whether or not a draft proposal is needed. Afterwards, and once the development of the draft proposal has been decided, the pre-publication is done, where comments from individuals are received; and, then, the draft proposal is published. However, there are no transparency mechanisms to make known the participation of all the stakeholders, as well as whether or not they had an impact on the draft proposal.

Chapter 7 includes specific recommendations for Peru to address each of these building blocks.

Note

[1] The PCM, MINJUSDH and MEF have officials devoted to carry out the RIA of the regulatory projects, on top of performing other functions.

Reference

OECD (2008), *Building an Institutional Framework for Regulatory Impact Analysis (RIA): Guidance for Policy Makers*, OECD Publishing, Paris, http://dx.doi.org/10.1787/9789264050013-en. [1]

Chapter 7. Recommendations to adopt the building blocks of a RIA system in Peru

The recommendations included in this chapter follow the framework set out in the report OECD (2008), Building an Institutional Framework for Regulatory Impact Analysis (RIA): Guidance *for* Policy Makers. *These recommendations result from evaluating the level of adoption in Peru of each of the building blocks of the RIA system, described in Chapter 6. The recommendations are also consistent with those included in the report* OECD (2016), Regulatory Policy in Peru: Assembling the Framework for Regulatory Quality. *Annex 7.A includes a priority proposal for the implementation of the recommendations contained in this chapter.*

Recommendations to introduce RIA

A political commitment to RIA, which includes getting support from stakeholders and establishing a legal mandate for RIA

1. Peru should issue a legally binding instrument that establishes the obligation for ministries and government entities issuing regulations to make an *ex ante* evaluation of the regulatory proposal, which includes at least the following elements:

- Definition of the public policy problem to be solved.
- Objective to be achieved through government intervention.
- Identification of alternatives to the regulation to address the public policy problem.
- Impact evaluation of each of the alternatives, and demonstration that the regulatory option is the one providing the greatest net benefit.
- The impact evaluation of the alternative corresponding to the regulation must include an estimate of the new formalities to be generated, including the measurement of potential administrative burdens. In this sense, the RIA system must integrate the current process of Regulatory Quality Analysis, so that there is only one system for the *ex ante* evaluation of the regulation.
- Early consultation measures taken.
- Definition of strategies to promote compliance with regulation, including the identification of resources for oversight tasks.
- Definition of strategies to monitor and evaluate the performance of regulations, including the definition of indicators to measure the degree of accomplishment of public policy objectives.
- The following chapter suggests model processes for the issuance of regulations that address each of these steps.
- Ideally, the criteria and guidelines suggested here should be part of the legislation and be specified in its Regulations and/or corresponding manuals.

The issuance of the Legislative Decree 1448 (see Chapter 4) which defines the policy of improving the quality of regulation and defines RIA as a tool for it, is an encouraging development in this direction. The PCM, MEF and MINJUSDH's publication of the implementation decree should consider addressing the recommendations made in this section.

2. In order to have the highest level of political commitment, the President of the Republic should endorse the legal instrument, so line ministries and their public entities sign up compliance with the RIA.
3. Define and execute an action programme to get the support from stakeholders that include ministries and public entities, universities, business associations and civil society, Congress, among others. This programme should include communication and training actions to inform these stakeholders about the benefits and challenges of the RIA system. It would also encourage the participation of such stakeholders in the consultation process of the rules recommended below.

Timely integration of RIA in the decision-making process

4. Include in the RIA manual to be published, diagrams and processes explaining in detail that RIA should be started in the early stages of the public policy design (see below specific recommendation). The next chapter suggests model processes for the issuance of regulations that address each step of the RIA process.

Build a RIA team inside the administration, including the creation of an institutional setting.

5. The OECD report *Regulatory Policy in Peru: Assembling the Framework for Regulatory Quality* (OECD, 2016[1]) recommends that:

As a first step, Peru could consider establishing a co-ordination council on regulatory policy in which the Ministry of Economy and Finance, the Presidency of the Council of Ministers, and the Ministry of Justice and Human Rights have permanent seats, and with sufficient capabilities to exercise an effective oversight function. Responsibilities and roles for each of the members would have to be defined clearly for the functioning of this council.

The Committee is already working, but without legal mandate. It is recommended to issue a legal instrument to vest it with legal personality, which should include the criteria under which the regulation will be evaluated.

6. The OECD report *Regulatory Policy in Peru: Assembling the Framework for Regulatory Quality* (OECD, 2016[1]) recommends that:

Peru should aspire at establishing an oversight body, which concentrates, if not all, most of the regulatory policy activities and tools currently spread across several ministries, agencies and offices. This oversight body should have the legal capability and the necessary resources to carry out an active enforcement of activities, while overseeing the complete regulatory policy, including the capacity to return draft regulation with a proper assessment through the use of regulatory impact analysis (RIA), when the defined criteria are not met.

Figure 7.1. Grounds upon which an oversight body can return RIA for revision

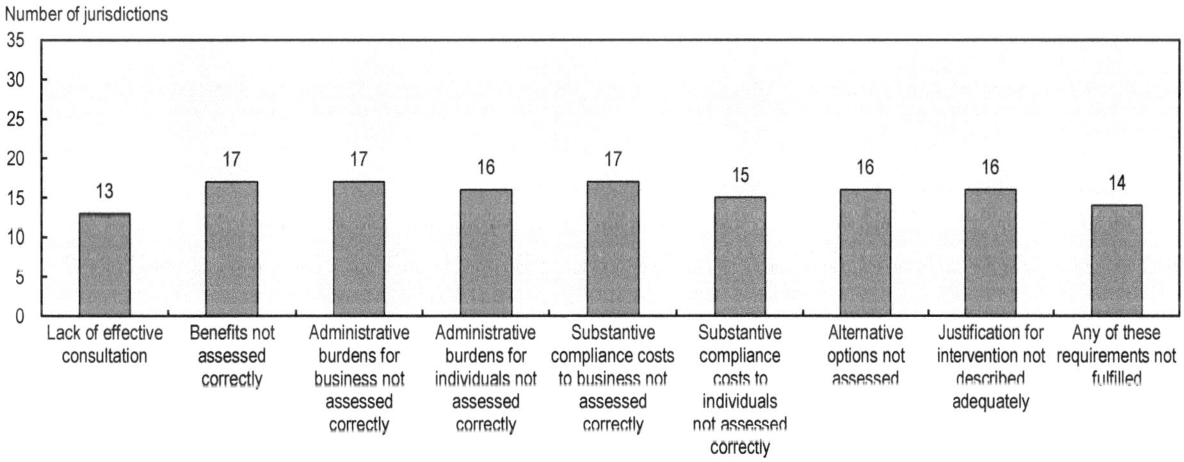

Notes: Based on data from 34 countries and the European Commission. The figure displays the number of countries that have reported the different grounds on which an oversight body can return RIA for revision for either primary laws or subordinate regulations.

Source: 2014 Regulatory Indicators Survey results, www.oecd.org/gov/regulatory-policy/measuring-regulatory-performance.htm, (OECD, 2015[2]), *OECD Regulatory Policy Outlook 2015*, Paris, http://dx.doi.org/10.1787/9789264238770-en.

7. The oversight body must have enough financial and human resources to perform its duties effectively. In particular, it must ensure that it has a cross-functional team with expertise in the areas of public policy, law and economics.
8. The oversight body should have the capability to reject regulatory proposals whose RIAs do not meet the required standards. This should be lay down in the legal instruments that establishes the RIA system and the oversight body (see international examples in Box 7.1 and Figure 7.1).

Box 7.1. Ensuring correct assessment of costs and benefits: some country examples

In Australia, a preliminary assessment determines whether a proposal requires a RIA and helps to identify best practice for the policy process. A RIA is required for all Cabinet submissions. There are three types of RIAs: long form, standard form and short form. Short form assessments are only available for Cabinet submissions. Both the long form and standard form must include, amongst other requirements, a commensurate level of analysis. The long form assessment must also include a formal cost-benefit analysis.

In Canada, for the case of subordinate regulations, when determining whether and how to regulate, departments and agencies are responsible for assessing the benefits and costs of regulatory and non-regulatory measures, including government inaction. This analysis should include quantitative measures and, if it is not possible to quantify benefits and costs, qualitative measures. When assessing options to maximise net benefits, departments are to: identify and assess the potential positive and negative economic, environmental, and social impacts on Canadians, business (including small business), and government of the proposed regulation and its feasible alternatives; and identify how the positive and negative impacts may be distributed across various affected parties, sectors of the economy, and regions of Canada. Treasury Board of Canada Secretariat provides guidance and a challenge function throughout this process.

In Mexico, RIAs are reviewed by the National Regulatory Improvement Commission (CONAMER) and if they are unsatisfactory, for example, by not providing specific impacts, CONAMER can request the RIA to be modified, corrected or completed with more information. If the amended RIA is still unsatisfactory, CONAMER can ask the lead ministry to hire an independent expert to evaluate the impact. The regulator cannot issue the regulation until CONAMER's final opinion.

In the United States, for the case of subordinate regulation, agency compliance with cost-benefit analysis is ensured through review of the draft RIA and draft regulation by the Office of Information and Regulatory Affairs under Executive Order 12866.

Source: (OECD, 2015[2]), *OECD Regulatory Policy Outlook 2015*, Paris, http://dx.doi.org/10.1787/9789264238770-en.

Recommendations for designing the RIA framework

Co-ordination and management

9. Consider the creation of official liaison units on regulatory policy within the ministries and entities that issue regulations, which serve to strengthen the organisation and co-ordination within the RIA system (see international examples in Box 7.2).
10. Consider the establishment of an electronic RIA management system to facilitate its operation and interaction between the ministries and entities that issue regulations and the oversight body.

Box 7.2. Network of officials for regulatory policy, examples from OECD countries

In the **United Kingdom** there is a central unit for better regulation. Better Regulation Executive, subordinated to the Department for Business, Energy and Industrial Strategy, is the agency responsible for the management of regulatory policy. This unit does not draw up rules or regulations, it is rather a core that interconnects the central government, the parliament, the National Audit Office, and the national regulatory bodies. Moreover, it identifies the official responsible for the process of better regulation in each ministry This agency exerts influence on several government areas.

In **Mexico**, the heads of the entities and decentralised agencies of the federal public administration appoint officials who act as better regulation liaisons before CONAMER; and they are assigned specific tasks within the better regulation process. They are in charge of co-ordinating and enforcing this process within their own entities and agencies, submitting to CONAMER the better regulation programme related to the regulations and procedures they implement, as well as of signing and sending both drafts – regulations and procedures – that should be subject to the process of better regulation. These liaison officials should be deputy ministers or chief administrative officers, that is, hold the next level after the incumbents, which strengthens the process.

Source: (OECD, 2010[3]), *Better Regulation in Europe United Kingdom*, http://dx.doi.org/10.1787/9789264084490-en; Cámara de Diputados del H. Congreso de la Unión (2017), Art. 69-H. Ley Federal de Procedimiento Administrativo Título Segundo del Régimen Jurídico de los Actos Administrativos, www.diputados.gob.mx/leyesbiblio/pdf/112_020517.pdf.

Targeting and prioritising RIA efforts

11. Define some list and/or criteria of the regulatory proposals that will be exempted from RIA, because they do not have any impact on regulated parties (see further information in Box 7.3). See in the next chapter the suggested model processes for the issuance of regulations that address the case of exemption from RIA.

Box 7.3. Cases of exemption from the RIA

There are several ways to determine whether a draft proposal requires preparing a RIA. Australia uses a list of questions that regulators must respond to prepare the RIA. The criterion in Mexico is that any provision generating costs above zero to users requires a RIA. The United States sets caps on monetary cost (OECD, 2015[2]).

It is possible that a regulatory proposal does not create costs to those subject to regulation. An obvious example is when a ministry or public entity wishes to implement a improvement measure of better regulation that may be:

- The elimination of an administrative procedure
- The elimination of requirements
- A decrease in response time
- The reduction of technical demands
- The removal of a ban

In these cases, regulated parties will benefit from the measure because there is a reduction in the costs of compliance with regulation.

In others, the very nature of the regulatory provision results in zero compliance costs to regulated parties because it does not impose any obligation on them. This type of provisions relates more to internal government processes, government transparency obligations, or to other legal obligations. Some examples are the following ones:

- Official appointment or dismissal of government officials
- Publication of opening hours for the public
- Working days of the entity, non-working days, or closing for vacation periods
- Change of location of public offices

It is possible to prepare a list of regulatory provisions that, a priori, do not require a RIA because it is expected that they will not impose any cost on regulated parties.

In these cases, it is advisable that the oversight body of better regulation keeps the power to demand the preparation of a RIA, even if a regulation might seem to fall in the cases of exemption.

12. Establish at least two types of RIA, one for high-impact regulatory proposals, for which a thorough and in-depth impact analysis must be done; and another for the remaining proposals, whose impact analysis be less substantial. The RIA manual should state the characteristics of the analysis to be performed for each case (see an example from Mexico in Box 7.4). See in the next chapter the suggested model processes for the issuance of regulations that address these cases.

Box 7.4. Exceptions to the Regulatory Impact Expression and types of analyses in Mexico

In **Mexico**, the Federal Law of Administrative Procedure (LFAP) provides for exempting the obligation to submit the Regulatory Impact Expression (MIR, for its nomenclature in Spanish) when the draft regulation does not create compliance costs on individuals. In this case, however, the relevant body should send to CONAMER the regulatory proposal accompanied by a request for exemption. This must confirm that the proposal does not fall into the following categories: i) it creates new obligations and/or penalties for individuals or tighten the existing ones; ii) it modifies or creates procedures that involve greater administrative burdens or compliance costs to individuals; iii) it reduces or restricts benefits or rights for individuals; iv) it establishes or modifies definitions, classifications, methodologies, criteria, characterisations, or any other reference term, affecting rights, obligations, benefits or procedures of individuals. By observing the above, the regulatory proposal may be exempted from submitting the corresponding MIR. In spite of this, CONAMER reserves its right to deny the exemption request and require the submission of the corresponding MIR, if considers that the regulatory proposal does generate compliance costs to individuals.

As of 2010, in Mexico there were the following types of regulatory impact assessment:

- **Moderate-impact MIR:** This MIR must be prepared when the potential impact of the draft regulation submitted before CONAMER is moderate, according to the result of the Regulatory Impact Calculator.
- **High-impact MIR:** This MIR must be prepared when the potential impact of the draft regulation submitted before CONAMER is high. This classification is determined through the Regulatory Impact Calculator.
- **Periodic-updating MIR:** This MIR is prepared in the case of draft regulations that intend to modify provisions, which, must be updated on a regular basis, without imposing additional obligations to those already existing.
- **Emergency MIR:** This MIR is prepared when the draft meets the following criteria to issue emergency regulation: i) if the measures proposed in the draft have a lifespan of no more than six months; ii) if it is designed to address an immediate harm or mitigate or eliminate an existing harm to the health or wellbeing of population, the environment, or natural resources; and iii) if emergency treatment has not been previously requested for a draft with equivalent content.

In November 2012, the following types of MIR were implemented in addition to the existing ones:

- **Moderate-impact MIR with competition impact analysis:** This MIR must be prepared when the Regulatory Impact Calculator rates the potential impact of the draft regulation submitted before CONAMER as moderate, and the result of the Competition Impact Checklist concludes that it may affect competition in markets.
- **High-impact MIR with competition impact analysis:** This MIR must be prepared when the Regulatory Impact Calculator rates the potential impact of the draft regulation submitted before CONAMER as high, and the result of the Competition Impact Checklist concludes that the draft contains actions that could impact the intensity of competition, economic efficiency and consumer welfare, either by restricting or promoting specific changes in market conditions.
- **High-impact MIR with risk analysis:** This MIR must be prepared when the Regulatory Impact Calculator rates the potential impact of the draft regulation submitted before CONAMER as high, and the result of the Competition Impact Checklist identifies actions intended to address, mitigate or lessen a risk.
- **High-impact MIR with competition impact analysis and risk analysis:** This MIR must be prepared when the result of the Regulatory Impact Calculator, the Competition Impact Checklist and the Risk Impact Checklist concludes that the potential impact of the draft regulation submitted is high, it identifies actions that could impact the intensity of competition, economic efficiency and consumer welfare, either by restricting or promoting specific changes in market conditions, as well as actions or measures intended to address, mitigate or lessen a risk.

- **MIR *ex post*:** This MR is prepared to review the regulation in order to determine the accomplishment of its objectives, as well as its efficiency, effectiveness, impact and permanence.

Later, in December 2016, the following ones were added:

- **Moderate-impact MIR with analysis of impact on foreign trade:** This MIR must be prepared when the result of the Regulatory Impact Calculator and the Foreign-Trade Impact Screening concludes that the potential impact of the draft regulation submitted before CONAMER is moderate, and provisions that may have an impact on foreign trade are identified.
- **High-impact MIR with analysis of impact on foreign trade:** This MIR must be prepared when the result of the Regulatory Impact Calculator and the Foreign-Trade Impact Screening concludes that the potential impact of the draft regulation submitted before CONAMER is high, and provisions that may have an impact on foreign trade are identified.
- **Moderate-impact MIR with competition impact analysis and analysis of impact on foreign trade:** This MIR must be prepared when the result of the Regulatory Impact Calculator, the Competition Impact Checklist and the Foreign-Trade Impact Screening concludes that the potential impact of the draft regulation submitted before CONAMER is moderate; and actions that could impact the intensity of competition, economic efficiency and consumer welfare, either by restricting or promoting specific changes in market conditions, as well as provisions that may have an impact on foreign trade are identified.
- **High-impact MIR with competition impact analysis and analysis of impact on foreign trade:** This MIR must be prepared when the result of the Regulatory Impact Calculator, the Competition Impact Checklist and the Foreign-Trade Impact Screening concludes that the potential impact of the draft regulation submitted before CONAMER is high; and actions that could impact the intensity of competition, economic efficiency and consumer welfare, either by restricting or promoting specific changes in market conditions, as well as provisions that may have an impact on foreign trade are identified.
- **High-impact MIR with risk analysis and analysis of impact on foreign trade:** This MIR must be prepared when the result of the Regulatory Impact Calculator, the Risk Impact Checklist, and the Impact on Foreign Trade Screening concludes that the potential impact of the draft regulation submitted before CONAMER is high; and actions or measures intended to address, mitigate or lessen a risk, and provisions that may have an impact on foreign trade are identified.
- **High-impact MIR with competition impact analysis, risk analysis, and analysis of impact on foreign trade:** This MIR must be prepared when the result of the Regulatory Impact Calculator, the Competition Impact Checklist, the Risk Impact Checklist, and the Foreign-Trade Impact Screening concludes that the potential impact of the draft regulation submitted before CONAMER is high, identifies actions that could impact the intensity of competition, economic efficiency and consumer welfare, either by restricting or promoting specific changes in market conditions; identifies actions or measures intended to address, mitigate or lessen a risk; and provisions that may have an impact on foreign trade are identified.

In all cases, and irrespective of the results of the Regulatory Impact Calculator, when CONAMER deems it appropriate, it may request, in writing, the preparation of a MIR other than the one submitted that include extensions and corrections.

Source: (OECD, 2014[4]), *Regulatory Policy in Mexico: Towards a Whole-of-Government Perspective to Regulatory Improvement*, Paris, http://dx.doi.org/10.1787/9789264203389-en; Ley Federal de Procedimiento Administrativo Título Segundo del Régimen Jurídico de los Actos Administrativos de México; CONAMER. (s.f.). Marco Jurídico, Comisión Federal de Mejora Regulatoria, Gobierno, gob.mx, www.gob.mx/conamer (accessed 23 January 2018).

13. Define the criteria and processes by which the oversight body will rate a regulatory proposal as moderate or high impact, which must be included —at least— in the corresponding RIA manual (see international examples of criteria to define the thoroughness of the RIA in Box 7.5).

Box 7.5. Threshold tests to apply RIA: Some country examples

In **Australia**, a Preliminary Assessment determines whether a proposal requires a RIA (or a RIS, regulation impact statement as they call it) for both primary and subordinate regulation (as well as quasi-regulatory proposals where there is an expectation of compliance). A Regulation Impact Statement is required for all Cabinet submissions. This includes proposals of a minor or machinery nature and proposals with no regulatory impact on business, community organisations or individuals. A RIA is also mandatory for any non-Cabinet decision made by any Australian Government entity if that decision is likely to have a measurable impact on businesses, community organisations, individuals or any combination of them.

Belgium applies a hybrid system. For example, of the 21 topics that are covered in the RIA, 17 consist of a quick qualitative test (positive / negative impact or no impact) based on indicators. The other 4 topics (gender, SMEs, administrative burdens, and policy coherence for development) consists of a more thorough and quantitative approach, including the nature and extent of positive and negative impacts.

Canada applies RIA to all subordinate regulations, but employs a Triage System to decide the extent of the analysis. The Triage System underscores the Cabinet Directive on Regulatory Management's principle of proportionally, in order to focus the analysis where it is most needed. The development of a Triage Statement early in the development of the regulatory proposal determines whether the proposal will require a full or expedited RIA, based on costs and other factors:

- Low impact, cost less than CAD 10 million present value over a 10-year period or less than CAD 1 million annually;
- Medium impact: Costs CAD 10 million to CAD 100 million present value or CAD 1 million to CAD 10 million annually;
- High impact: Costs greater than CAD 100 million present value or greater than CAD 10 million annually. Also, when there is an immediate and serious risk to the health and safety of Canadians, their security, the environment, or the economy, the Triage Statement may be omitted and an expedited RIA process may be allowed.

Mexico operates a quantitative test to decide whether to require a RIA for draft primary and subordinate regulation. Regulators and line ministries must demonstrate zero compliance costs in order to be exempt of RIA. Otherwise, a RIA must be carried out. For ordinary RIAs comes a second test – qualitative and quantitative – what Mexico calls a "calculator for impact differentiation", where as a result of a 10 questions checklist, the regulation can be subject to a High Impact RIA or a Moderate Impact RIA, where the latter contains less details in the analysis.

New Zealand employs a qualitative test to decide whether to apply RIA to all types of regulation. Whenever draft regulation falls into both of the following categories, then RIA is required: i) the policy initiative is expected to lead to a Cabinet paper, and ii) the policy initiative considers options that involve creating, amending or repealing legislation (either primary legislation or disallowable instruments for the purposes of the Legislation Act 2012).

The **United States** operates a quantitative test to decide to apply RIA for subordinate regulation. Executive Order 12866 requires a full RIA for economically significant regulations. The threshold for "economically significant" regulations (which are a subset of all "significant" regulations) is set out in Section 3(f)(1) of Executive Order 12866: "Have an annual effect on the economy of USD 100 million or more or adversely affect in a material way the economy, a sector of the economy, productivity, competition, jobs, the environment, public health or safety, or State, local, or tribal governments or communities."

In the **European Commission**, a qualitative test is employed to decide whether to apply RIA for all types of regulation. Impact assessments are prepared for Commission initiatives expected to have significant economic, social or environmental impacts. The Commission Secretariat general decides whether or not this threshold is met on the basis of reasoned proposal made by the lead service. Results are published in a roadmap.

Source: (OECD, 2015[2]), *OECD Regulatory Policy Outlook 2015*, Paris, http://dx.doi.org/10.1787/9789264238770-en.

14. The oversight body must keep power to change the thoroughness of the RIA, regardless of the above-mentioned definition process.

Data collection

15. The RIA manual should include a section detailing and listing the public sources of data and information that could be used to carry out the corresponding assessment.
16. The RIA manual must define alternative strategies for data collection in the event of unavailability of data, such as surveys or meetings with stakeholder groups. It should be emphasised that in the early consultation stage (see recommendations on early consultation below) there are plenty of possibilities for gathering information, which, ultimately, will allow to conduct a correct assessment of public policy proposals (for more information on how to obtain the data to conduct RIA, see Box 7.6).

Box 7.6. How to obtain the data needed for a RIA: basic concepts

Obtaining high quality data is a basic challenge to conduct a RIA. Without good data, RIA will contribute relatively little to good policy-making. However, data collection can be a time-consuming and expensive exercise. This means that a careful and strategic approach must be adopted. The following are data collection strategies that should be considered when commencing a RIA and should be carefully weighed according the particular RIA project. As many of these data collection methods may require considerable resources, it may be necessary to rely on third party sources to obtain information, which saves time and research costs.

Surveys

By designing a questionnaire, specific information on major elements of a proposed regulation can be asked. A well-designed survey of affected groups can provide a good basis for estimating the costs of compliance. However, care is needed in several areas:

- The survey should be sent to a representative group of affected parties, trying to ensure that all the main groups who will have to comply with the regulation are included.
- The questionnaire must be realistic. This means the questions should be carefully considered to ensure that respondents provide meaningful answers. Conducting a trial with a very small number of respondents can help to identify potential problems related to this need.
- The sample size must be carefully considered. On one hand, a sufficient number of respondents is needed to trust on the identified trends; on the other, it must be ensured that the scale is not too demanding of scarce resources.
- It should try to guard against biased answers: those who must comply with regulations will have an interest in over-stating the costs of compliance. Careful design of the questions can guard against this problem.

Particularly where compliance costs are complex, one may wish to consider direct interviews as a way of improving the quality of the data received. Remember that surveys covering relevant issues may have been completed previously, either by government or by other bodies. It should try to identify relevant survey results that are already available to improve existing knowledge and reduce the costs of data collection.

Business test panel

An innovation pioneered in Denmark is the Business Test Panel, a list of companies that have agreed to assist government in conducting RIA. These companies volunteer to advice on the likely costs of regulatory proposals. This group is used as the basis for administering surveys. This model has the advantage that, over time, the business involved will become familiar with the RIA concept and gain a better understanding of the nature of the questions being asked and the information that is needed. It needs to be ensured, however, that the answers received are not biased by the fact that a particular "insider" group is questioned on a frequent basis.

Review of experience in other countries

In many cases, a similar regulation to the one being considered may have been adopted in neighbouring countries. Contacting government officials, or other sources, in those countries can be an effective way of obtaining information on the likely impacts of your regulatory proposal.

Other government agencies

A large amount of relevant data is held by government agencies. For example, the government statistical office is a rich source of general information on issues such as the number of firms in various industries, the number of people employed and the like. Other useful material may also be available within government. For example, regulations with similar features may previously have been adopted.

Literary reviews

Reviewing the existing academic literature can be a very interesting way of obtaining relevant information. The Internet can increasingly be used to conduct literature searches; likewise, market reports and other research documents commissioned by industry associations or similar groups can be very useful. For example, insurance companies may have much relevant data on the size and nature of the harms that regulations try to prevent. This can be used to estimate the size of likely regulatory benefits.

Source: (OECD, 2008[5]), "Introductory Handbook for Undertaking Regulatory Impact Analysis (RIA)", Paris, https://www.oecd.org/gov/regulatory-policy/44789472.pdf (accessed 3 August 2017).

17. The RIA manual must consider the possibility of commissioning data collection for high-impact RIAs to external firms.
18. Regarding the high-impact RIA, the requirement of conducting a cost-benefit monetary analysis should be laid down in the RIA manual (see a summary of the cost-benefit analysis methodology in Box 7.7).

Box 7.7. Summary of the cost-benefit analysis methodology

The cost-benefit analysis (CBA) is one of the approaches used to measure the impacts of a regulatory proposal. This six-step methodology proposes the quantification (in monetary terms) of the costs and benefits of the regulation. Implementing this methodology involves:

- Identifying the direct and indirect impacts of the alternatives to the regulation. This step also includes a distributional analysis and a competition impact analysis, as well as specific information about compliance costs, including the administrative burden that can be measured through the Standard Cost Model.
- Quantifying and monetising costs and benefits. Allocating a monetary value can be based on market prices (if available) or on alternative approaches such as hedonic prices, defense costs, travel costs, or contingent valuation.
- Defining the appraisal horizon and determining cash flows. The number of periods that will be employed to assess the costs and benefits of the proposal can be established in various ways. In general, the number of years in which the contribution of discounted costs and benefits begins to be minimal is considered; however, the expected life of capital investments or the duration of the programme could also be used.
- Discounting flows. This step involves establishing a discount rate in order to update cash flows to present value. This step and the previous one are particularly important because they determine the net present value of the proposal and, hence,

its preference or not over another. The present value is calculated by discounting the cash flows (both costs and benefits) with the following formula:

$$V_0 = \frac{V_t}{(1+r)^t}$$

Where:

V0: Present value
Vt: Monetary value in the period
r: Discount rate
t: Number of periods

Once the flows have been discounted, the benefits are added and the costs subtracted. Although costs tend to be identified at the beginning of the proposal, this is not necessarily always the case; so, it is important to consider all expenses and benefits during the life of the regulation. The proposal with the highest net present value should be preferred.

- Sensitivity analysis (if necessary). The sensitivity analysis involves making changes in relevant variables to see how the results change. This process is important when regulatory proposals have different periods or in which it is difficult to determine a discount rate.
- Choosing the best alternative. Once the evaluation criteria are available, it is necessary to choose the intervention to be carried out. The alternative with the highest net benefit or that with a higher cost-benefit ratio (and greater than 1) is frequently chosen.

The cost-benefit analysis is an objective way to evaluate the impact of a regulation; there may be discrepancies, however, when determining the discount rate or allocating a monetary value to intangible elements (for example, satisfaction).

Source: (COFEMER, 2013[6]), "Guía para Evaluar el Impacto de la Regulación", www.cofemer.gob.mx/presentaciones/espa%f1ol_vol%20i.%20metodos%20y%20metodologias_final.pdf; (European Commission, 2017[7]), "Better regulation Toolbox", https://ec.europa.eu/info/sites/info/files/better-regulation-toolbox.pdf.

19. As to moderate-impact RIAs, the RIA manual should state that —apart from the cost-benefit analysis— other methodologies can be used. This can include cost-effectiveness analysis, multi-criteria decision-making analysis (see a summary of other methodologies available for impact evaluation in Box 7.8). It also must state that the qualitative identification of the costs and benefits of each alternative should be included, as a minimum.

Box 7.8. Summary of other methodologies for the impact evaluation

Cost-effectiveness analysis

The cost-effectiveness analysis (CEA) is mainly used in those cases where it is very expensive to conduct a cost-benefit analysis. The CEA allows comparing, in monetary terms, the costs with the benefits that cannot be monetised. That is, this methodology quantifies the benefit for each monetary unit allocated to the proposal. Like the CBA, the cost-effectiveness analysis follows a series of steps in its preparation.

- Quantifying the costs of each regulatory alternative. In this first step, direct and tangible costs are determined for each policy option.
- Quantifying the benefits of each regulatory alternative. In this case, benefits are not measured in monetary terms, but accounted using alternative measures according to the objective of the program. For example, measures such as increased life expectancy, the amount of CO_2 emissions that is reduced, or the level of educational attainment can be used to estimate the benefits.
- Quantifying the effectiveness for each option. The cost-effectiveness ratio, defined as the net present value of costs divided by benefits, is the criterion used to determine the preference of one option over another.
- Choosing the regulatory alternative with the lowest cost-effectiveness analysis.

Multi-criteria decision-making analysis

This method consists in weighing and analysing the different evaluation criteria, it is particularly useful in cases where the economic, social and environmental dimensions are relevant. The building blocks of this methodology are the following ones:

- Setting the objectives to be evaluated. It consists in identifying the main purpose of the policy, as well as the secondary goals.
- Identifying the evaluation criteria. This is particularly important because the necessary parameters to weigh the accomplishment of the objectives set in the previous step are defined. The selected indicators must be mutually exclusive, that is, a criterion cannot influence on more than one indicator.
- Identifying the options to be evaluated. A small set of alternatives must be evaluated, but with different options, in order to analyse policies with substantially different effects.
- Rating and evaluating the expected performance from each option, according to the evaluation criteria that was chosen. As the evaluation can be quantitative or qualitative, it is important to make that results be comparable to each other, in order to obtain a single result from every policy option considered. The standardisation of results is carried out with a scale from 0 to 100 (where 0 is the less desirable result and 100 is the most favorable one).
- Weighing of criteria. Once results are standardised, it is necessary to generate a single indicator for each policy alternative. The construction of the indicator implies determining the relative importance of individual evaluation criteria, which may be the responsibility of the regulatory body or an external advisor.
- Combining the weights and scores of each option. The final score of each of the alternatives considers is the weighted average of all the criteria evaluated.
- Choosing the policy alternative with the highest score.

Source: (COFEMER, 2013[6]), "Guía para Evaluar el Impacto de la Regulación", www.cofemer.gob.mx/presentaciones/espa%f1ol_vol%20i.%20metodos%20y%20metodologias_final.pdf; (European Commission, 2017[7]), "Better Regulation Toolbox", https://ec.europa.eu/info/sites/info/files/better-regulation-toolbox.pdf.

20. Establish that, in both types of RIA, the analysis must include an assessment of the new procedures created, including the measurement of potential administrative burdens.

Consultation, participation and transparency

21. Lay down in the legal mandate creating the RIA system that consultation is an essential element and specify that the regulatory proposals – as defined in the manual to be issued – must follow the two stages of the consultation: the early consultation and the consultation once the proposals is available.

22. Lay down in the RIA manual the necessary guidelines to establish the early consultation as a flexible and open, but necessary process (see more information on early consultation in Box 7.9).

Box 7.9. Early consultation: basic elements

The early consultation takes place when there is a problem that justifies government intervention. This consultation is good, fundamentally, to obtain information that allows identifying in a correct way the policy problem, its scale, and importance. At present, it is advisable to conduct a focused consultation that considers the main affected parties and those who can provide better information. This stage is prior to the design and submission of a regulatory proposal, that is, there is not yet a draft regulation; and, on the contrary, this consultation helps to define the possible form of government intervention to address a public problem.

The early consultation must be carried out as soon it is identified the need to step in, so that it helps to determine if government intervention is really needed – besides getting information and evidence of the identified problem. Moreover, above all, to guarantee how government must step in, defining if it will be through a regulatory proposal or by other mechanisms.

The European Commission proposes some types of methods and tools to carry out the early consultation, which are shown below, as example:

Method	Description
Focus groups	A discussion group of people with similar background or experiences focused on a specific topic that interests them.
Conferences, public hearing, activities with stakeholders	Direct interaction with a large number of stakeholders where varied information is collected
Meetings, workshops and seminars	Direct interaction with a limited number of stakeholders where specific information is collected.
Interviews	Tool for gathering information via in-depth conversations with one or several individuals.
Questionnaires	Tool for gathering information, usually written, that can be used in any consultation method, and had to be tailored to the purpose of the consultation and the group intended to consult.

Source: (European Commission, 2017[7]), "Better Regulation Toolbox", https://ec.europa.eu/info/sites/info/files/better-regulation-toolbox.pdf.

23. Lay down in the RIA manual a standardised process for the consultation stage of the regulatory proposal, which must have the following characteristics:

- The regulatory proposal and the corresponding RIA should be made available for consultation for a minimum of 30 business days.

- Those subject to regulations should be able to comment on both the regulatory proposal and the RIA.
- The Ministries and entities issuing regulations must reply all comments and, at the end of the process, issue a document summarising all the comments received and the actions that will be taken to address the relevant ones.

24. Create an online system for the consultation stage of the regulatory proposal and the corresponding RIA (see the example of Mexico in Box 7.10) that:

- Centralises and includes all regulatory proposals and the corresponding RIA under consultation.
- Allows regulated parties to send their comments, and that they are made public.
- Allows ministries and entities issuing regulation to reply to the comments, and that they are made public.
- Allows ministries and entities issuing regulations to publish the document that summarise all the comments received and the actions that will be taken to address the relevant ones.

Box 7.10. The consultation in the Regulatory Impact Assessment in Mexico

Consultation in Mexico is strongly influenced by the requirements formally established in two separate pieces of legislation. First, the Federal Lay of Administrative Procedures sets out specific public consultation requirements as an integral part of the RIA process. Second, more recently adopted transparency legislation has established more general consultation requirements that are independent of the RIA process itself. In particular, this law requires all regulatory proposals to be published on the website of the relevant ministry or regulatory agency.

The RIA process itself provides important public consultation opportunities, as well as important safeguards to ensure that adequate account is taken of comments received from stakeholders. In particular, the CONAMER publishes in their website www.conamer.gob.mx all draft RIA as soon as they are received, as well as its comments on the draft RIA and all inputs received from stakeholders. This generalised publication of a wide range of RIA-related documentation is possibly unique among OECD member countries. Importantly, publication of CONAMER's response to the draft RIA provides stakeholders with additional information that can potentially allow them to participate more effectively in the process.

For example, by highlighting weaknesses in the analysis, this material may assist stakeholders to identify data or other materials they possess which could be fed into the analysis to enhance its quality. More generally, the publication of all stakeholder comments on the proposal provides the basis for a more detailed dialogue on its merits among interested parties. The CONAMER believes that the publication of this wide range of RIA-related documents is a key factor in ensuring that regulators take account of CONAMER's opinions and, hence, that it is a critical success factor for the RIA process.

The draft RIA is required to be open to consultation for at least 20 working days but, in practice, much longer consultation periods appear to be the norm. This reflects, in part, the need for the CONAMER to undertake its initial analysis of the RIA document and publish its response. Consequently, it appears that the process provides extensive opportunities for stakeholder input. The CONAMER also supports effective engagement in consultation by actively providing the draft RIA to key stakeholders and soliciting their inputs in many cases.

Source: (OECD, 2014[4]), *Regulatory Policy in Mexico: Towards a Whole-of-Government Perspective to Regulatory Improvement*, Paris, http://dx.doi.org/10.1787/9789264203389-en.

25. In the case of multisectoral regulatory proposals, the consultation process should be carried out before the revision of the Vice-Ministerial Coordination Council (CCV).

Recommendations to prepare RIA implementation

Development of guidelines

26. Issue a guide for the simplified RIA that currently performs the MEF-PCM-MINJUSDH Committee for the *ex ante* impact evaluation of regulatory proposals. This guide might include an impact checklist and guidelines for its response. See an international example in Box 7.11.

Box 7.11. The Regulatory Criteria Checklist of British Columbia, Canada

In British Columbia, Canada, the Regulatory Criteria Checklist (RCC) replaced the Regulatory Impact Assessment (RIA) in 2001. Ministers and heads of regulatory authorities must make sure that any proposed legislation, regulation and new policy are evaluated according to the criteria set out in the checklist. A signed copy of the RCC or exemption form must be included with any legislation submitted for Executive Council review and any Order in Council that is being recommended by the responsible minister to the Executive Council to enact a regulation. Copies of the signed RCC and exemption forms must be provided to Straightforward BC. In addition, the responsible minister or head of a regulatory authority must make the RCC available to the public, at no charge, on request.

The RCC itself is simple and includes several questions in eleven different categories: i) reverse onus: need is justified; ii) cost-benefit analysis; iii) competitive analysis; iv) streamlined designed; v) replacement principle; vi) results-based designed; vii) transparent development; viii) time and cost of compliance; ix) plain language, x) simple communications and xi) sunset review/expiry principle.

Each category has a yes/no checkbox next to it. If the answer to the questions in any category is "no", then an explanation must be attached. At the end of the form, there is a box that asks how many regulatory requirements will be added and how many will be eliminated, as well as what the net change will be. When the reform policy was first introduced in 2001, two regulatory requirements had to be eliminated for every one introduced. Since 2004, when the original goal to reduce regulation by one-third was met, a target of no net increase has been in place and extended to 2015. The RCC encouraged a change in culture from one where regulation was seen as the answer to any problem and the private sector was viewed with some suspicion, to one where questions are asked, alternatives are considered, and the contributions that businesses make to the economy is better understood.

Source: (García Villarreal, 2010[8]), "Successful Practices and Policies to Promote Regulatory Reform and Entrepreneurship at the Sub-national Level", *OECD Working Papers on Public Governance*, No. 18, Paris, http://dx.doi.org/10.1787/5kmh2r7qpstj-en.

27. Once issued the legal instrument that establishes the RIA system, issue the RIA manual.

28. This manual must include, at least, the following sections:

- The public policy process and when each RIA stage must be carried out (see suggested model processes to issue regulations in Chapter 8).
- List of criteria or instruments exempted from RIA.
- Process to perform the analysis that allows identifying the thoroughness of the analysis of the RIA.
- Instructions to fill out each section of the RIA form for high-impact RIAs, including an explanation on the methodology of the Cost-Benefit Analysis.
- Instructions to fill out each section of the RIA form for moderate-impact RIAs, including an explanation on the methodologies of the Cost-Effectiveness Analysis and the Multicriteria Decision-Making Analysis.
- Instructions to carry out the early consultation.
- Guide with information about data sources.

Training the regulators

29. Design and deliver a training programme for communicating the RIA timetable implemented by the MEF-PCM-MINJUSDH Committee, and fill out the simplified RIA according to the guide above recommended.

30. Once issued the legal instrument that establishes the RIA system, implement a recurrent training program.

31. This programme must include different levels of complexity in the courses (for example, induction courses vs. advanced courses), according to the demand of officials, the training needs, and the objectives of the oversight body.

32. In addition to the training program, seek exchanging technical internships with the OECD countries for the adoption of good practices in respect of RIA. In these internships, officials from the oversight body and from the ministries and government entities issuing regulations might participate, according to the objectives set out by the oversight body.

Communication as a tool for RIA, including the communication within the public administration and report the results

33. Once issued the legal instrument that establishes the RIA system, implement a programme of public meetings to communicate the progress of the RIA system, and supplement it with the preparation of public and regular progress reports.

Annex 7.A includes a proposal of priority implementation of the recommendations.

References

COFEMER (2013), *Guía para Evaluar el Impacto de la Regulación*, http://www.cofemer.gob.mx/presentaciones/espa%f1ol_vol%20i.%20metodos%20y%20metodologias_final.pdf. [6]

European Commission (2017), *Better regulation Toolbox*, https://ec.europa.eu/info/sites/info/files/better-regulation-toolbox.pdf. [7]

García Villarreal, J. (2010), "Successful Practices and Policies to Promote Regulatory Reform and Entrepreneurship at the Sub-national Level", *OECD Working Papers on Public Governance*, No. 18, OECD Publishing, Paris, https://dx.doi.org/10.1787/5kmh2r7qpstj-en. [8]

OECD (2016), *Regulatory Policy in Peru: Assembling the Framework for Regulatory Quality*, OECD Reviews of Regulatory Reform, OECD Publishing, Paris, https://dx.doi.org/10.1787/9789264260054-en. [1]

OECD (2015), *OECD Regulatory Policy Outlook 2015*, OECD Publishing, Paris, https://dx.doi.org/10.1787/9789264238770-en. [2]

OECD (2014), *Regulatory Policy in Mexico: Towards a Whole-of-Government Perspective to Regulatory Improvement*, OECD Reviews of Regulatory Reform, OECD Publishing, Paris, https://dx.doi.org/10.1787/9789264203389-en. [4]

OECD (2010), *Better Regulation in Europe: United Kingdom 2010*, Better Regulation in Europe, OECD Publishing, Paris, https://dx.doi.org/10.1787/9789264084490-en. [3]

OECD (2008), *Introductory Handbook for Undertaking Regulatory Impact Analysis (RIA)*, https://www.oecd.org/gov/regulatory-policy/44789472.pdf. [5]

Annex 7.A. Proposal of roadmap for the implementation of the recommendations

Recommendations with priority proposal

Priority	Recommendation
1	5. Issue a legal instrument to give legal formality to the RIA pilot programme committee.
1	26. Issue a guide for the simplified RIA currently being conducted by the MEF-PCM-MINJUSDH Committee for the *ex ante* impact review of draft regulations.
2	1. Issue a legally binding instrument for the RIA system.
2	2. The legal instrument should have the support of the President of the Republic.
	Contents of the legal instrument:
	11. Define a list and/or criteria of the regulatory projects that will be exempted from RIA.
	12. Establish at least two types of RIA, one for high-impact normative projects, and one for all other projects.
	13. Define the criteria and process by which the oversight body will decide when a regulatory project is of moderate impact, and when it is of high impact.
	21. Stipulate the consultation process as an essential element in the legal instrument creating the RIA system, and specify that draft regulations, as defined in the manual to be issued, must comply with the two stages of consultation.
3	27. Once issued the legal document establishing the RIA system, issue the RIA manual.
	Contents of the RIA manual:
	28. Definitions of the sections of the RIA Manual
	4. Include that RIA should be initiated in the early stages of the public policy design.
	15. The RIA manual shall establish a section identifying and listing the public sources of data and information.
	16. The RIA manual should define options for data collection strategies when data is not available.
	17. The RIA manual should consider the possibility of commissioning external offices to collect data for high-impact RIAs.
	18. For high-impact RIA, the RIA manual should stipulate the requirement to conduct a cost-benefit monetary analysis.
	19. For moderate-impact RIAs, stipulate in the manual that, in addition to the cost-benefit analysis, other methodologies may be used.
	20. Establish that, in both cases of RIA, the analysis must include an evaluation of the new procedures generated.
	23. Stipulate in the RIA Manual a standardised process for the consultation stage of the normative project.
	25. For multisectoral policy projects, the consultation process should be implemented prior to the CCV revision.
4	29. Design and implement a training programme to publicise the RIA calendar.
4	30. Once the legal document establishing the RIA system is issued, implement a recurring training program.
	31. Such a programme should include different levels of complexity (e.g. introductory courses vs. advanced courses).
	32. In addition to the training programme, seek technical exchange visits with OECD countries for the adoption of good RIA practices.
4	33. Once issued the legal document establishing the RIA system, implement a programme of public meetings to communicate the progress of the AIR system.
4	10. Consider establishing an electronic RIA management system
4	24. Create an online system for the consultation phase of the draft standard and the corresponding RIA.
4	9. Consider creating official regulatory policy liaison points within ministries and entities.
4	3. Define and implement a programme of actions to gain stakeholder support.

Recommendations with permanent priority

6. Establish a supervisory body that concentrates most regulatory policy tools and activities.
7. The oversight body should have adequate financial and human resources.
8. The oversight body must have the ability to reject regulatory proposals where the RIA does not meet the required standards.

Chapter 8. Model processes to issue regulations in Peru

This chapter includes proposals of model processes for issuing regulations to conduct a high-impact RIA, a moderate-impact RIA, and the process of exemption from RIA for Peru. In each case, the essential steps that must be included are explained.

In this chapter, proposals for processes to issue regulation in Peru are made, and the steps of the RIA are specified.

There are several compelling reasons to be clear about the model process for the issuance of regulations. First, it ensures that the RIA be an essential part of the public policy process, so that RIA provides adequate information to make an evidence-based decision. The RIA compels officials to think critically about the existing problem, define whether or not government action is necessary, consider the available public policy alternatives to address the problem, determine if regulation is the best option, conclude whether the regulation would produce greater benefits than costs, identify the building blocks to implement effectively the regulation, and ensure that the opinions from stakeholders and affected parties are taken into account.

Second, it provides clarity about when the different RIA steps in the process to issue regulations must be carried out, in order to guarantee that RIA is initiated from the early stages of the public policy process, and that it contributes effectively to make the best decision. What should be avoided is to add the RIA as a further step at the end of the public policy process, once the decision to regulate has already been made. In this case, the purpose of RIA of contributing to issue quality regulations based on evidence becomes null.

Finally, the model processes for issuing regulations can help to implement the proportionality criterion within RIA, which assumes that the exhaustiveness of the assessment to be conducted must be proportional to the impact foreseen in the regulation. Considering that government resources are scarce and conducting a RIA requires significant resources, it is advisable that – for regulations in which a high impact is expected – the responsible officials should carry out a more sophisticated analysis that includes monetising the benefits and costs. Instead, when it comes to regulations with limited impact, the thoroughness of the analysis must be defined with less demanding parameters.

Proposals for three types of model processes are set out below: high-impact RIA, moderate-impact RIA and exemption from the RIA.

High-impact RIA

Figure 8.1 contains a flowchart of the model process for the high-impact RIA proposal. The steps suggested are the following ones:

1. Potential public-policy problem arises

The public policy cycle starts here. Ministries or government entities realise, by different means, that there is a potential problem, which may require government action through the design and execution of a public policy.

It is possible that from the moment the potential public-policy problem arises, co-ordination is required among different areas within a ministry, among different ministries or government entities. Occasionally, the very nature of the potential problem can indicate which areas of government should be involved. Therefore, from this stage it must be evaluated if it is necessary to start the co-ordination among different areas of government.

Figure 8.1. Proposal for the high-impact RIA process

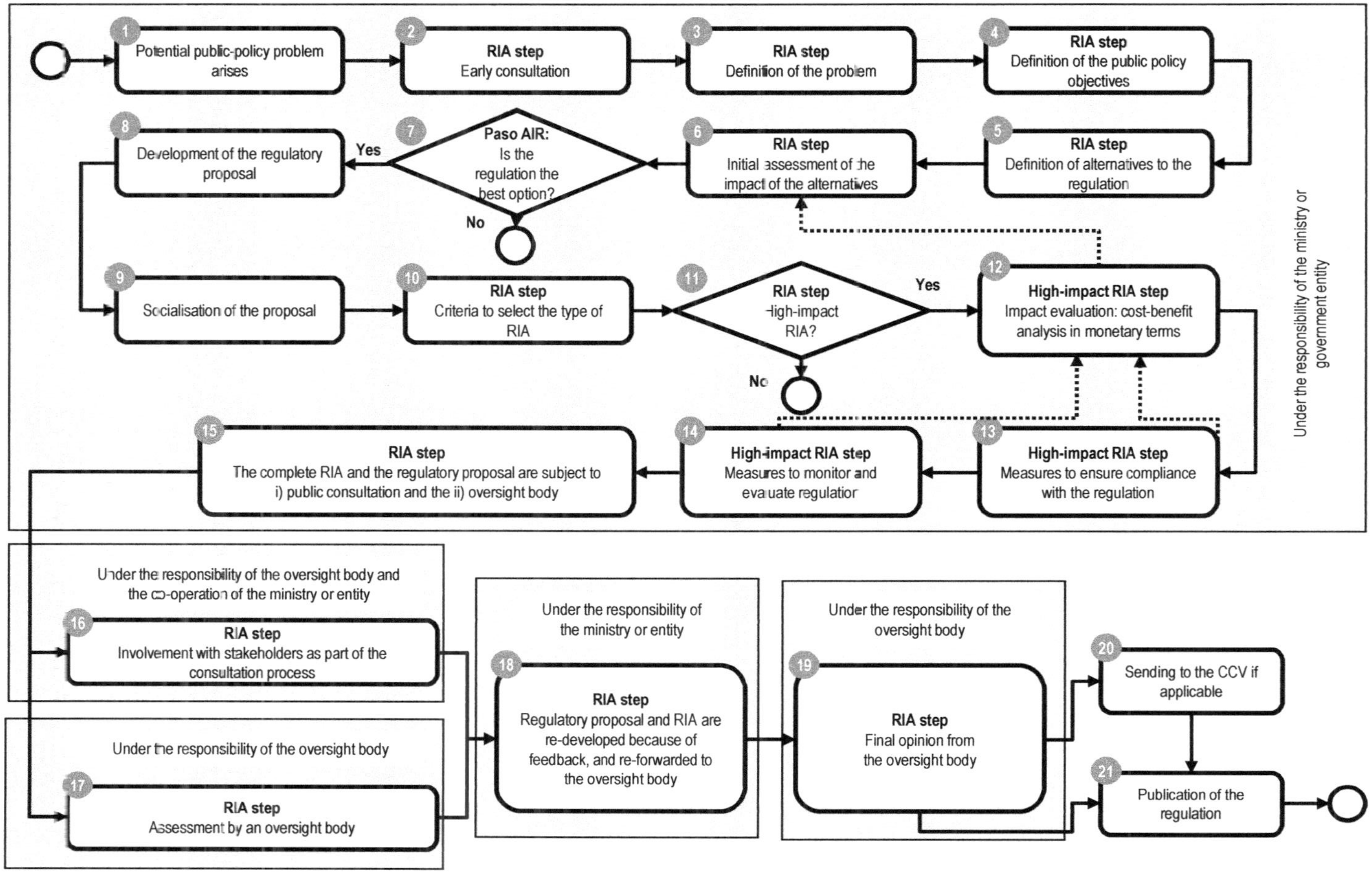

2. RIA step: early consultation

The RIA process starts formally here. Once the potential problem has been identified, it is advisable that ministries or entities conduct an early consultation with stakeholders. This consultation can be useful to determine if there is really a problem and, should it be the case, define its scale, resolve whether or not government action is needed, and identify possible ways of addressing it.

If at this stage there is still no co-ordination among the different areas within a ministry, or among ministries or government entities, it is possible that the need to establish such co-ordination arises as a result of the early consultation. That will depend on the information collected.

See Chapter 7 for more detailed information about the nature of the early consultation.

3. RIA step: definition of the problem

At this stage, ministries or government entities must clearly define the nature of the problem to be solved. Ideally, the early consultation should provide information to define the problem based on evidence. If the consultation is not performed, it would be necessary to get the evidence from other sources.

The correct definition of the problem can lead to conclude that co-ordination with other areas of government is necessary, if it has not yet begun, so that the following steps are carried out jointly.

See Box 8.1 for further information on how to define the problem.

Box 8.1. Definition of the problem in the RIA process

The identification of the problem is the first and most important step. If the problem is incorrectly defined, the rest of the RIA will not be sufficient to establish an appropriate regulatory program. Consequently, even if a basic RIA is performed, it is imperative to conduct a good analysis to identify the problem. To facilitate the categorisation of the elements that must be included in the definition of the problem, the following can be taken into account: delimitation, cause and effect, and scale.

The delimitation of the problem must address a first context of the problem that was perceived. Certain aspects of the problem must be defined in this stage. First of all, the concrete definition of the problem, where the question should be addressed, why is it problematic? Although occasionally it may seem intuitive, an exercise to develop an explicit definition must be carried out to lay concrete foundations for the rest of the RIA. To have a full perspective of the situation, it also needs to be defined if there are related problems. Lastly, the delimitation must include a baseline to assess the problem. This will serve both to set the objectives and to evaluate the regulation that be implemented.

Once the problem intended to be solved is identified, attention should be focused on assessing its size and nature. This means to determine:

- What groups of society are being affected;
- The size of each group;
- What is the nature of the impact on each group;

- How big are the impacts, and
- For how long would these impacts persist.

All the effects on the different groups should be considered when defining the size of the problem, based on the context of the objective intended to be accomplished.

4. RIA step: definition of the public policy objectives

In this section of the RIA, ministries and government entities must devote themselves to define the objective to be accomplished by way of government action, using as a starting point the problem to be addressed. As in the previous step, the early consultation can provide inputs and information to fulfill this step.

The correct definition of the public policy objectives can lead to conclude that co-ordination with other areas of government is necessary, if it has not yet begun, so that the following steps are carried out jointly.

See Box 8.2 for further information on how to define the public policy objectives.

Box 8.2. Definition of public policy objectives in the RIA process

Once the problem is identified, specific objectives must be set out to address its root causes. The RIA can contribute to make regulations as effective and efficient as possible. An effective regulation accomplishes the objectives it was devised for. A regulation is effective if it accomplishes those objectives at the lowest cost for all society groups.

The efficiency and effectiveness are important as there are always limits in the number and type of regulations that can be absorbed by society and implemented effectively by governments. Regulation always imposes costs and offers benefits, and if it is inappropriate it may distort economic growth by hampering the way businesses are done and creating negative perceptions about the economic environment. At the same time, making and implementing regulations demands important resources from governments; that is why it is essential that it be well designed.

How to improve efficiency and effectiveness through RIA?

The decision-making process to draw up regulations can be improved by using the RIA. Particularly, RIA helps to promote a systematic decision-making process and a comparative approach to that decision making. The RIA makes officials think about the following questions and answer them:

- Generally, what is the problem that we must solve?
- What is the objective that we want to accomplish?
- What are the available means to accomplish that objective?

Before proposing any regulation, these questions should be raised. By starting the whole process with these questions, it is almost certain that as many practical options as possible can be identified to accomplish the objective, which is fundamental in the case of looking for the best option.

A very common mistake is to start the analysis by confusing "means" and "ends". The public-policy or regulatory objective is the "final result" that the government wants to achieve. This should not be confused with the "means" to reach it because, then, there would be no capacity to consider the merit of all the alternatives that may exist. For instance, a public policy objective can be to reduce the number of deaths due to traffic accidents. Reducing the speed limit is a means to achieve the goal, but it is not the goal itself. Other means may be to require particular safety measures or to improve road conditions. This example shows that there are several ways and options to achieve the goal.

After all possible options have been identified, the RIA must be compared in terms of benefits and costs. It means that attempts should be made to identify all the impacts from the different options. Once this is done, each and every option can then be analysed to get information on which is the most effective and efficient.

Maximising social welfare

Regulation should proceed only if it is expected to improve the economic conditions of society and its welfare. This is only accomplished if the total benefits of a regulation – for society as a whole – are greater than the total costs, considering all the impacts on society. An important dimension that RIA must consider is that "society as a whole" should always be taken into account, instead of paying too much attention to the impacts on certain groups, who might push for to get a specific regulatory decision made.

SMART objectives

The following characteristics prepared by the European Commission (Specific, Measurable, Achievable, Realistic, Timely, SMART), which are explained below, can be taken into account to develop sound objectives:

Specific: the objective must be concrete enough so that it is not open to interpretations and seek to address specific problems and not macroeconomic situations.

Measurable: a monitoring and evaluation plan must be considered at this point in the RIA; therefore, it is necessary to set an objective that can be evaluated in order to analyse if the implemented regulation is working.

Achievable: it is necessary to set out objectives that can reasonably be accomplished, avoiding optimist biases that end up by making them unfeasible.

Realistic: the objective must explicitly relate to the problem and its causes.

Timely: the timeframes in which the objectives are to be achieved in order to design the evaluation must be specified.

Source: Adapted from (European Commission, 2015[1]), "Better Regulation Guidelines", p. 65, http://ec.europa.eu/smart-regulation/guidelines/docs/swd_br_guidelines_en.pdf.

5. RIA step: definition of alternatives to the regulation

Once the problem and the objective to be achieved with government intervention are defined, ministries and entities must determine the different alternatives available to address the problem and achieve the objectives set out. In this case, the early consultation can also provide information and input to define the alternatives.

It should be noted that the regulatory option is only one of the possible alternatives, and that other non-regulatory alternatives should be included as possible resources to address the problem and accomplish the objective.

See Box 8.3 for further information on how to identify the alternatives.

Box 8.3. Definition of alternatives to the regulation in the RIA process

Normally, regulation is the only option considered by decision-makers, perhaps because there is a very old habit in the government of favouring this tendency. However, it is necessary to consider alternatives to identify if the public policy problem can be addressed in another way, depending on its specific circumstances.

Other intervention tools can be those mentioned below:

- To conduct an information campaign to inform or prevent the public about a problem;
- To offer specific information directly to consumers so they look after their own interests.
- To force those who offer goods or services to give information to consumers before they purchase the products;
- To impose a tax to discourage an activity;
- To grant a subsidy to stimulate a particular behaviour;
- To promote the development of a "self-regulation" scheme within the industry or a particular group.

6. RIA step: Initial assessment of the impact of the alternatives

In this step, ministries and government entities must perform an initial assessment of the costs and benefits of each of the alternatives identified. In the case of the regulatory alternative, it is not necessary to have the regulatory proposal completely drawn up. An outline of the regulation would suffice to meet this requirement.

With the problem well defined, and with the objectives intended to achieve, it should be possible to do an analysis of the net benefits expected from each option. The analysis should not be exhaustive, but rather a guide to decide if proceeding with the regulatory option is the most advisable alternative. It means that, while a full monetary cost-benefit analysis should not be pursued, at least a well-justified qualitative analysis or some other impact evaluation technique should be carried out (see options for evaluation techniques Chapter 7).

It must be taken into account that the RIA is a recursive process: as the ministry or entity advances in preparing the RIA, more information is collected and the evaluation process is perfected and refine; which should lead to carry out another assessment of the alternatives. The final decision to issue or not a regulation will depend on the result of reevaluating the options constantly.

See further information on step 6, initial assessment of the impact of the alternatives in Box 8.4.

Box 8.4. Initial assessment of the impact of the alternatives in the RIA process

In many cases, the initial analysis done through the RIA may indicate that it is not desirable to regulate. Other type of tool can allow us to achieve the goals we pursue in a more efficient and effective way. In those cases, RIA can help because it gives more insight into the possible impacts of alternative approaches to regulation to achieve public policy objectives. Or, the analysis performed may reveal that government intervention is not necessary.

Discovering that it is not necessary to do something to solve the problem can occur in the following cases:

- When the size of the problem is so small that the costs of government action are not justified, and
- When the analysis proves that a regulation, or any other action, is not feasible to effectively address the problem and at a reasonable cost that allows to get some kind of benefit.

How can one conclude that regulation is justified?

There is no specific rule to determine if the problem is big enough to justify government action. However, the following elements can be considered:

- The limited capacity of government to enforce regulations effectively;
- The size of the problem compared to others that, it was considered, needed regulations;
- The capacity of the affected groups to take some action that can solve the problem,
- If the problems tend to last for a long time, or if they can change relatively quick because of external factors.

Once all these elements are taken into account, if the regulation is thought to be justified, it must be considered whether the regulation will solve the problem at a reasonable cost compared to other alternatives.

7. RIA step: Is the regulation the best option?

Once the different alternatives have been evaluated, it is decided whether or not the option of issuing a regulation is the best. This assessment assumes that there is enough evidence to reach a reliable conclusion. If the assessment performed with the evidence and information available suggests that the regulatory option is the most desirable because of the potential net benefits it generates, then the next step must be carried on. Otherwise, the most feasible alternative must be examined with the greatest thoroughness. As more information is collected and the degree of complexity of the RIA increases, this assessment must be repeated.

8. Development of the regulatory proposal

It is advisable to prepare in detail the regulatory proposal until an initial assessment of the alternatives has been made, and that the regulatory option be validated as the one that can potentially provide the greatest net benefits.

The necessary internal steps must be carried out in this stage, so that the technical areas from the ministries and government entities co-ordinate with the legal offices to decide on the type of legal instrument that will be drawn up. Involving the legal departments must also guarantee the legality of the rule, as well as compliance with technical legal requirements, such as those provided for in the *Guide on Legislative Technique for the Development of Regulatory Proposals from the Entities of the Executive Branch,* from the MINJUSDH.

In this step, it is advisable that the technical areas of the ministries or entities share with the legal teams the content of the RIA created so far, which must include:

- Definition of the problem;
- Definition of the public policy objectives;
- Identification of the alternatives;
- Initial assessment of the alternatives;
- Description of the early consultation process, its results and input to each of the previous sections.

The purpose of this is that all legal departments know the information, evidence and assessment that led to the decision of drawing up a regulatory proposal and, thus, ensure the alignment of the objectives that are sought through the regulation between the technical areas and the legal departments.

9. Diffusion of the proposal

Depending on the nature of the problem, the public policy objective and the type of regulation intended to be issued, co-ordination among the government offices, ministries or entities must already have taken place.

If it has not started, the responsible ministry or entity must establish – in this step – the co-ordination with the appropriate agencies. It is possible that steps 8 and 9 are carried out simultaneously, because the preparation of the regulatory instrument is usually made jointly. But, for didactic purposes, in this report the two steps are shown sequentially.

10. RIA step: criteria to select the type of RIA

The previous chapter recommends that Peru implements the proportionality criterion within RIA: the thoroughness of the assessment of the regulatory option must be consistent with the expected impact of said regulation (see recommendations 12 and 13).

In this step, entities and ministries should apply the criteria previously established by the oversight body regarding regulatory policy, to decide on the type of RIA that must be prepared and submitted (see international examples of differentiation criteria among the types of RIA, in Box 7.5).

The decision on the type of RIA —high-impact or moderate-impact— will define the content of the impact evaluation sections (step 12), the measures to ensure compliance with the regulation (step 13), and the measures to monitor and evaluate regulation (step 14), as explained below.

11. RIA step: high-impact RIA?

Should the criteria be met, ministries or government entities will prepare the high-impact RIA.

12. High-impact RIA step: impact evaluation, cost-benefit analysis in monetary terms

For high-impact RIA, it is advisable to perform a monetary analysis of the costs and benefits. Considering the high impact expected from the regulation, the description of benefits needs to be thorough with values expressed in monetary terms. Likewise, it must be proven that the benefits from the regulatory proposal are greater than the costs.

See a summary of the methodology and more bibliography in Box 7.7.

Additionally, it must be proven that, among the alternatives considered, the regulatory proposal is the one offering the greatest net social benefit. For this, the benefits and costs of the alternatives identified in step 5 must be reevaluated, and a general reassessment must be made to decide which alternative offers the highest net benefits. For this reason, Figure 8.1 includes a feedback link between this step and step 6. Should the regulatory option be the one with the highest expected net social benefit, the process to issue the regulation would continue.

13. High-impact RIA step: measures to ensure compliance with the regulation

An essential part of the regulatory governance cycle is to implement and enforce regulation, as illustrated in Figure 1.4. For this reason, in this step, ministries and government entities must detail the proposed strategies to maximise the compliance by regulated parties with the obligations established in the regulatory proposal.

Box 8.5 includes further information on the measures to ensure compliance with the regulation.

Box 8.5. Measures to ensure compliance with the regulation in the RIA process

Making a realistic analysis of the compliance rate expected to achieve with the regulatory proposal is an important element for evaluating the impacts. Regulation will only have an impact if people comply with it.

Compliance is a subject that should be studied from two points of view. First, if the evaluation considers that the risk of noncompliance is high, the reason for such a case must be studied. That will allow to weigh all the aspects of regulation that can be changed to promote compliance and it may mean changing the regulation substantially or modifying the communication or the proposed implementation.

Second, if there is a high risk of noncompliance, it must be considered if it is appropriate to continue with the regulatory proposal. Should a risk of regulatory failure be identified, because the regulation cannot remedy the market failure or solve the identified problem, or the cost of doing the latter is too high, it is advisable to stop and think whether it is worth continuing.

Several elements must be taken into account when thinking about the level of compliance. First, how to get that potentially affected groups voluntarily comply with the proposal. This is easier if regulation is reasonable and legitimate, if the cost of doing so in that way is not very high, or if the noncompliance would lead to major problems. The groups that tend to comply voluntarily are those that abide by the law.

Second, consider how efficient the inspection and oversight actions will be to increase the compliance rate. This means establishing if there are enough resources that can be used for such purpose and be able to detect problems at the appropriate time.

Third, consider whether it is valid to apply sanctions to those who fail to comply and if those sanctions will suffice to modify their behaviour, in order to increase the degree of compliance.

In general, if compliance rates tend to be low, it is essential to be able to detect or reduce noncompliance through implementation actions. If this cannot be done, then a failure in regulation may occur. It means reconsidering the regulatory proposal and check if there is an alternative mechanism that could be more effective.

As part of the high-impact RIA, it is advisable to define the following:

- Detailed programme of oversight and inspection tasks, including specific information on the resources needed to implement and operate the system.
- Detailed programme of sanctions and penalties for noncompliance, and the necessary resources to implement and operate the system.
- Detailed description of other measures that will be employed to increase the compliance rate, such as information campaigns, agreements with enterprise chambers, among others; and the necessary resources to implement and operate these measures.

The costs and benefits identified in this step must be included in the impact evaluation, which would compel to reassess the net benefit expected from the regulatory proposal; hence, a feedback link is included between this step and step 12 which, in turn, should lead to a comprehensive reassessment of the alternatives to address the public policy problem.

14. High-impact RIA step: measures to monitor and evaluate regulation

Ministries and entities must define, in this step, the measures that will be established to check the performance of regulation. These measures must include information and indicators to calculate the progress in the accomplishment of the public policy objective to be achieved through the regulation. The information and defined indicators must be clear enough so ministries or entities, as well as the public at large, notice that the problem identified in step 3 is addressed by applying the regulation, and to what extent the public policy objective defined in step 4 is achieved.

Additionally, the indicators that will allow evaluating the performance of regulation after a certain period of being applied must be defined in this step. In order to close the regulatory governance cycle, it is necessary to ensure that the public policy objectives set to be achieved at the outset —by issuing and applying the regulation— be truly accomplished. This evaluation must be carried out after a fairly long period that allows to appreciate the impact of regulations and that offers, at the same time, the opportunity of making the necessary amendments to regulations, including its elimination, if the objectives are not accomplished or that the public policy problem disappeared. Some OECD countries generally use a 3 to 5-year period to carry out the so-called *ex post* evaluation of regulations (OECD, 2015[21]).

In this step, the ministries or government entities must define *a priori* the information and indicators to be used in the *ex post* evaluation. The indicators to assess the regulation may or may not coincide with the monitoring indicators.

See further information on how to define the measures to monitor and evaluate regulation in Box 8.6.

Box 8.6. Measures to monitor and evaluate regulations in the RIA process

Monitoring of regulation

Monitoring is a systematic process to collect, analyse and use information to measure the progress in the achievement of the public policy objectives set in the regulatory proposal. Monitoring a regulatory proposal allows to identify if the regulation is being applied as expected or, as appropriate, if there is a need for implementing other measures. In order to carry out an adequate monitoring of our regulatory proposal we need to identify:

- What evidence do we need?
- When and how it must be collected?
- Who must collect it and from whom will it be obtained?

To this end, we must establish indicators that allow us to measure the performance of the regulatory proposal. These indicators must be defined, they must be measurable and measured in a given time. We must consider the following characteristics to obtain the information:

- The search for information must be exhaustive, that is, we must consider both qualitative and quantitative information.
- The cost of data collection must be proportional to the benefit expected by obtaining that information.
- To avoid requesting duplicate information, particularly, information that has been previously requested.
- The collection and use of the collected information should be timely; otherwise, it entails the risk that the information be useless and an excessive cost be generated.
- Last, transparency and the usefulness of information must be guaranteed during this process.

Evaluation of regulation

The evaluation of existing policies through the *ex post* impact analysis is necessary to ensure that regulations are effective and efficient. In some circumstances, the formal processes of the *ex post* impact analysis can be more effective than the *ex ante* analysis to inform about the ongoing policy debate. This may be the case, for instance, if regulations are drawn up under pressure to implement a rapid response. At an early stage of the public policy cycle, attention should be paid to the performance criteria for the *ex post* evaluation, that includes reviewing whether the objectives of regulation are explicit, what data will be used to measure performance, as well as the allocation of institutional resources. It can be difficult to allocate scarce public policy resources to review an existing regulation; likewise, it is necessary to systematically schedule the review of the regulation to ensure that the *ex post* evaluation be performed.

In order to carry out an *ex post* evaluation it is necessary, first, to identify and collect information on indicators that allow to measure the degree to which objectives have been accomplished, as well as the level of compliance and the effects of the regulation. These indicators should normally be determined in the framework of an *ex ante* evaluation, when applying some of the methods established to calculate the impacts (cost-benefit analysis, cost-effectiveness analysis, multicriteria decision-making analysis, among others).

The *ex ante* evaluation and the *ex post* evaluation are similar in the sense that the quality of regulation is assessed in both processes. Nevertheless, while the *ex ante* evaluation performs a probabilistic exercise to calculate the possible impacts that a future regulation will have once it is implemented, the *ex post* evaluation involves a verification exercise that requires gathering the information about compliance and the effects on the operators or regulation market during a certain period.

Thus, while the *ex ante* evaluation aims to predict the impact of a regulation based on a prospective analysis; the *ex post* evaluation is defined as a critical appraisal, supported by evidence, of whether a regulation meets the needs it intends to satisfy, and if it achieves the expected effects. The *ex post* evaluation goes beyond to assess whether or not something happened, it focuses on assessing the causality (that is, whether the action taken modified behaviours and produced the expected changes, or both).

The following must be defined in the high-impact RIA:

- Detailed plan to collect the necessary information and create the relevant indicators to measure the monitoring of regulation performance, including the periodicity of the collection and specific information on the resources needed to implement and operate the system.
- Detailed strategy for the *ex post* evaluation of regulation, including the collection and creation of indicators while the regulation is implemented to subsequently prepare the assessment, the periodicity of collection, and specific information on the resources needed to implement and operate the system.

Once this step is defined, the ministries or government entities must reevaluate the expected costs and benefits of the regulation which, in turn, must lead to a reassessment of the regulatory proposal to confirm whether it is the best public policy alternative.

15. RIA step: The complete RIA and the regulatory proposal are subject to i) public consultation and the ii) oversight body

Once all the sections of the RIA are completed and the regulatory proposal finalised, both must be sent to the public consultation process and the oversight body of regulatory policy.

16. RIA step: Involvement with stakeholders as part of the consultation process

In this step, the regulatory proposal and its RIA are made available to the public for review and comment. According to recommendation 23 of the previous chapter, consultation must have the following characteristics:

- The regulatory proposal and the corresponding RIA should be made available for consultation for a minimum of 30 business days.
- Regulated parties should be able to comment on both the regulatory proposal and the RIA.
- The Ministries and agencies issuing regulations must reply all comments and, at the end of the process, issue a document summarising all the comments received and the actions that will be taken to address the relevant ones.

The experience of the Ministry of Environment (MINAM), documented in Chapter 5, can be useful to implement this system.

17. RIA step: assessment by an oversight body

Simultaneously with the previous step, the oversight body of regulatory policy would review whether the RIA meets the criteria established in the respective guidelines. According to recommendation 8, the oversight body should have the capability to reject regulatory proposals whose RIAs do not meet the required standards.

18. RIA STEP: regulatory proposal and RIA are redeveloped due to the feedback, and reforwarded to the oversight body

In this step, the ministries and government entities must modify both the RIA and the regulatory proposal, using as input the information from the consultation process as well as the remarks by the oversight body.

19. RIA step: final opinion from the oversight body

The oversight body reassesses the draft RIA and the modified regulatory proposal, sent by the ministries and government entities and delivers its final opinion.

20. Sending to the CCV if applicable

In this step, the regulatory proposals with an impact on several sectors of the economy would be reviewed by the CCV as it currently happens. It should be noted that the report *Regulatory Policy in Peru: Assembling the Framework for* Regulatory *Quality* (OECD, 2016[3]) recommends that:

> *...the regulatory impact assessment should be part of the assessment from the CCV. The analysis that has to be carried out by the MEF, the PCM and the MINJUSDH should be done before the draft regulation goes to the Vice-ministerial Coordinating Council, with an adequate period to carry out the analysis. The opinion issued by the Coordination Council on Regulatory Policy or the oversight body on the draft regulation and the RIA should be considered as part of the assessment of the CCV.*

21. Publication of the regulation

This step includes all the applicable administrative and legal processes that currently exist in Peru prior to the publication in the *Official Gazette El Peruano*, such as the approval of the Council of Ministers for certain types of regulations.

Moderate-impact RIA

Figure 8.2 contains a flowchart of the model process for the moderate-impact RIA proposal. As the steps listed below are the same as the ones for the high-impact RIA, it is not necessary to repeat their description:

1. A potential public-policy problem arises
2. RIA step: early consultation
3. RIA step: definition of the problem
4. RIA step: definition of the public policy objectives
5. RIA step: definition of alternatives to the regulation

6. RIA step: initial assessment of the impact of the alternatives
7. RIA step: Is regulation the best option?
8. Development of the regulatory proposal
9. Diffusion of the proposal
10. RIA step: criteria to select the type of RIA
11. RIA step: moderate-impact RIA?

Should the criteria be met, the ministries or government entities will prepare the moderate-impact RIA.

12. Moderate-impact RIA step: impact evaluation, cost-benefit analysis in monetary terms

As opposed to the high-impact RIA, in the case of the moderate-impact RIA is appropriate to perform a qualitative cost-benefit analysis, or resort to another impact evaluation technique that be less demanding to express in monetary terms the benefits and costs.

Figure 8.2. Proposal for the moderate-impact RIA process

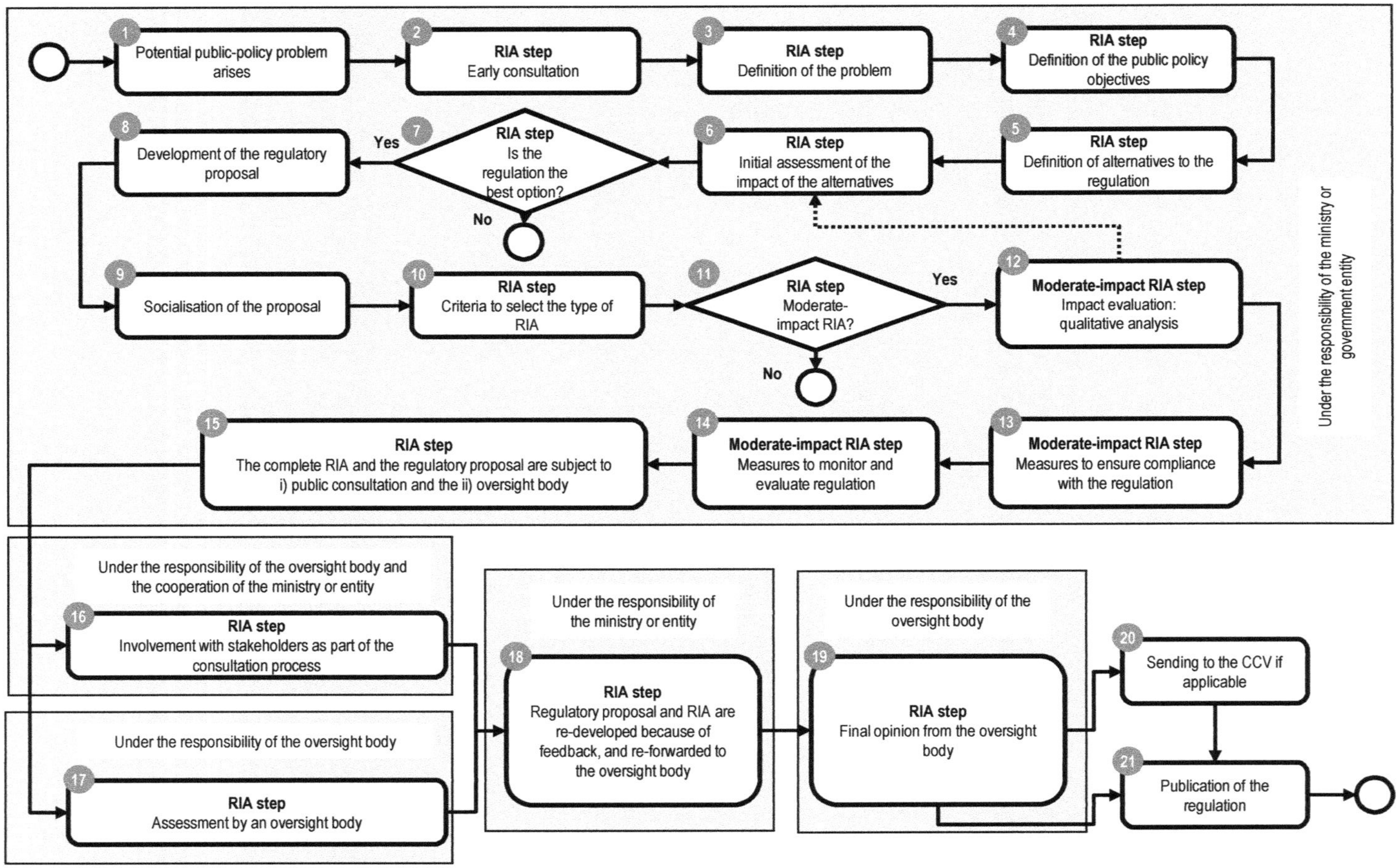

Doubtlessly, the cost-benefit analysis should always be the preferred option; but given the nature of the regulatory proposal of moderate impact, other techniques as the cost-effectiveness analysis or the multicriteria analysis are adequate. See further details in Box 7.8.

In any case, when it comes to moderate-impact regulatory proposals, a detailed qualitative description of the benefits and costs should be included.

As in the case of high-impact regulatory proposals, it should be proven that, among the alternatives considered, the regulatory proposal is the one offering the greatest net social benefits. For this, the benefits and costs of the alternatives identified in step 5 must be reevaluated, and a general reassessment must be made to decide which alternative offers the highest net benefits. For this reason, Figure 8.2 includes a feedback link between this step and step 6. If the regulatory option is the one with the highest expected net social benefit, the process to issue the regulation would continue.

13. Moderate-impact RIA step: measures to ensure compliance with the regulation

An essential part of the regulatory governance cycle is to implement and enforce regulation, as illustrated in Figure 1.4. For this reason, in this step, ministries and government entities must describe in a general way the proposed strategies to maximise compliance by regulated parties with the obligations stated in the regulatory proposal.

Box 8.5 includes further information on the measures to ensure compliance with the regulation.

As part of the moderate-impact RIA, it is advisable to define the following:

- General strategy of oversight and inspection tasks;
- Description of the programme of sanctions and penalties for noncompliance,
- Description of other measures that will be used to increase the compliance rate, such as information campaigns, agreements with enterprise chambers.

14. Moderate-impact RIA step: measures to monitor and evaluate regulation

In this step, ministries and entities must describe the measures that will be established to check the performance of regulation. These measures must include information and indicators to calculate the progress in the accomplishment of the public policy objective to be achieved through the regulation. The information and defined indicators must be clear enough so ministries or entities, as well as the public at large, notice that the problem identified in step 3 is addressed by applying the regulation, and to what extent the public policy objective defined in step 4 is achieved.

Additionally, the indicators that will allow evaluating the performance of regulation after a certain period of being applied must be defined in this step. In order to close the regulatory governance cycle, it is necessary to ensure that the public policy objectives set to be achieved at the outset – by issuing and applying the regulation – are truly accomplished. This evaluation must be carried out after a fairly long period that allow to appreciate the impact of regulations and that offer, at the same time, the opportunity of making the necessary amendments to regulations, including its elimination, if the objectives are not accomplished or that the public policy problem disappear. Some OECD countries generally use a 3 to 5-year period to carry out the so-called *ex post* evaluation of regulations (OECD, 2015[4]).

In this step, the ministries or government entities must define *a priori* the information and indicators to be used in the *ex post* evaluation. The indicators to assess the regulation may or may not coincide with the monitoring indicators.

See further information on how to define the measures to monitor and evaluate regulation in Box 8.6.

The following must be defined in the moderate-impact RIA:

- Detailed plan to collect the necessary information and create the relevant indicators to measure the monitoring of regulations performance, including the periodicity of the collection.
- Detailed strategy for the *ex post* evaluation of regulations, including to collect and create indicators while the regulation is implemented to subsequently prepare the assessment, and the periodicity of the collection.

As the steps listed below are the same as the ones for the high-impact RIA, it is not necessary to repeat their description:

15. RIA step: The complete RIA and the regulatory proposal are subject to i) public consultation and the ii) oversight body

16. RIA step: involvement with stakeholders as part of the consultation process

17. RIA step: assessment by an oversight body

18. RIA STEP: regulatory proposal and RIA are redeveloped because of feedback, and reforwarded to the oversight body

19. RIA step: final opinion from the oversight body

20. Sending to the CCV if applicable

21. Publication of the regulation

Exemption from RIA

This report presents two proposals for the RIA exemption process: for regulatory proposals that do not create costs to regulated parties, and for draft proposals included in an exemption list. Both are explained below.

Exemption from RIA for draft proposals included in an exemption list

The suggested process for the exemption from RIA for draft proposals included in an exemption list is shown in Figure 8.3. This process assumes the existence of the exemption list mentioned in recommendation 11. See some examples that could be included in that list in Box 7.3.

The process includes the following steps:

1. Development of the regulatory proposal

The very nature of the normative provisions that could be included in the exemption list implies zero compliance costs to regulated parties. Consequently, it is possible to expect that for this type of regulatory proposal it is not necessary to go through the steps of identification of the problem, definition of objective, and so on. On the contrary, it is certain to assume that the process begins with the development of the proposal.

2. Diffusion of the proposal

According to the type of regulation intended to be issued, the ministry or entity responsible establishes the co-ordination with the appropriate entities. It is possible that the steps 1 and 2 are carried out simultaneously, because the preparation of the regulatory instrument is usually made jointly. However, for didactic purposes, in this report the two steps are shown sequentially.

3. RIA step: criteria for the exemption from RIA

The previous chapter recommends that Peru must establish criteria for the exemption from RIA, that includes a list of regulatory proposals, which could be exempted from the Regulatory Impact Assessment (see recommendation 11).

4. RIA step: Is the regulatory proposal included in the list?

Should the regulatory proposal be in the exemption list, the ministries or government entities must prepare the request for the exemption from RIA. The list should be as detailed as possible in order to avoid ministries and agencies using loopholes to be exempted from carrying out the RIA.

5. Exemption from RIA step: to prepare and send the request for the exemption from RIA

The ministry or government entity prepares the request for the exemption from RIA and sends it to the oversight body for its assessment.

6. Exemption from RIA step: assessment of the request

The oversight body assesses the exemption request. First, it must verify whether the normative provision is actually in the list. Second, even if the normative provision is in the list, the oversight body must determine whether it does or does not create any cost for regulated parties.

Only when both criteria are met, the oversight body must issue the exemption approval. In any other case, it must ask to the ministry or entity to prepare a RIA.

If the latter occurs, and considering that there is already a regulatory proposal, it would be advisable that the ministries or government entities begin the process of preparing the RIA in the step 3 of the moderate-impact RIA or high-impact RIA, taking into account that the first part of both processes is the same.

As the steps listed below are the same as the ones for the high-impact/moderate-impact RIA, it is not necessary to repeat their description:

7. Sending to the CCV if applicable

8. Publication of the regulation

Figure 8.3. Suggested process to exempt from RIA draft proposals included in an exemption list

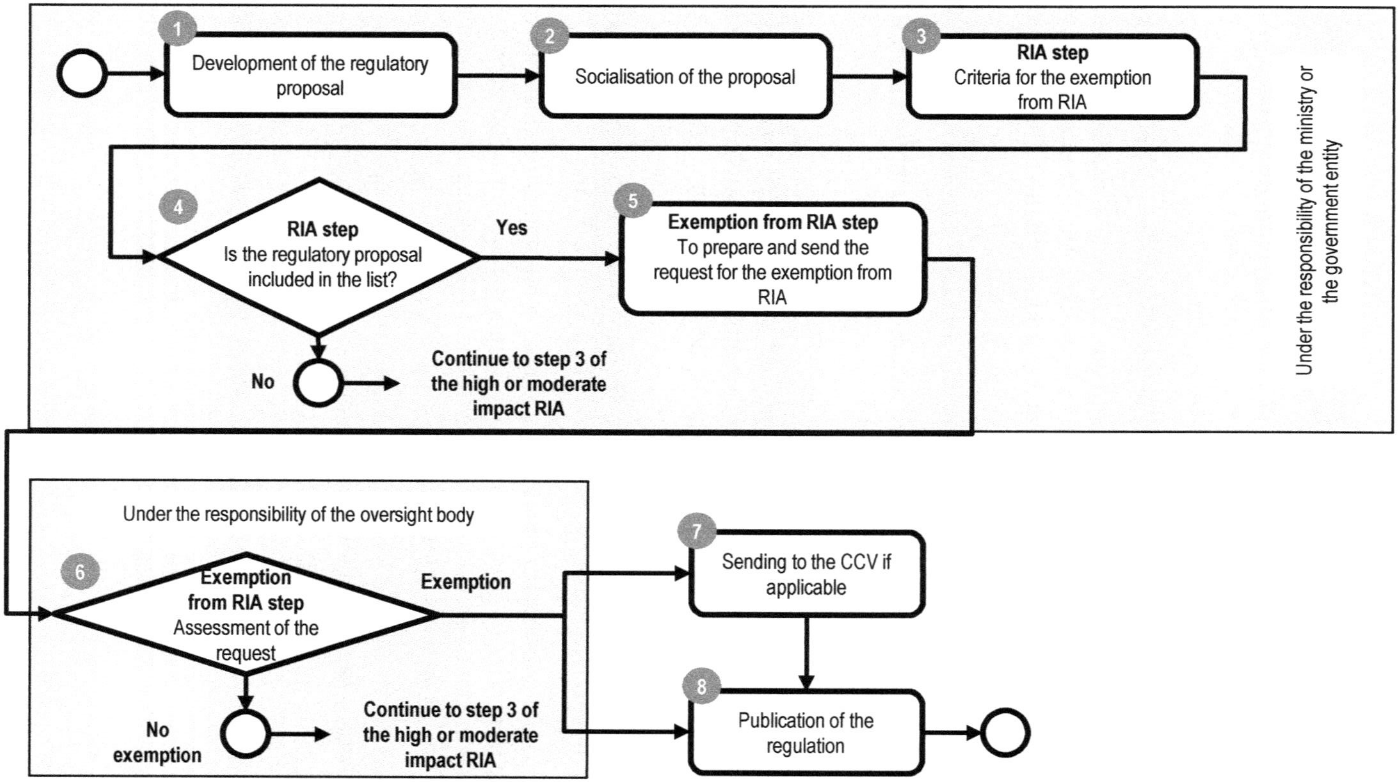

Exemption from RIA for regulatory proposals that do not generate costs to regulated parties

It is possible that a regulatory proposal does not generate costs to regulated parties (see some examples in Box 7.3). In those cases, the model process suggested to request the exemption from RIA is shown in Figure 8.4.

As the steps listed below for this process are the same as the ones for the high-impact/moderate-impact RIA, it is not necessary to repeat their description:

1. Potential public-policy problem arises

2. RIA step: early consultation

3. RIA step: definition of the problem

4. RIA step: definition of the public policy objectives

5. RIA step: definition of the alternatives to the regulation

6. RIA step: initial assessment of the impact of the alternatives

RIA step: Is regulation the best option?

8. Development of the regulatory proposal

9. Diffusion of the proposal

The aforementioned steps are expected to be the same as the ones for the standard RIAs, because the proposals falling into the no-costs assumption may be legitimately attempting to solve a public policy problem. Hence, the importance of following the steps mentioned above.

10. Exemption from RIA step: criteria for the exemption from RIA

The previous chapter recommends that Peru must establish criteria for the exemption from RIA, that includes the criterion of exempting normative provisions not generating costs to regulated parties (see recommendation 11).

11. Exemption from RIA step: Does the regulatory proposal generate costs?

In this step, the ministry or government entity must be in a position to determine whether or not the regulatory proposal generates costs to regulated parties. Specifically, once step 6 is performed – "Initial assessment of the impact of the alternatives" – ministries or government entities are able to determine if the normative provision meets the criteria of zero compliance costs. Should it be the case, the exemption request must be prepared. Otherwise, step 11 of high impact or moderate impact RIA must be followed to determine the thoroughness of the analysis.

12. Exemption from RIA step: to prepare and send the request for the exemption from RIA

The ministry or government entity prepares the request for the exemption from RIA and sends it to the oversight body for its assessment.

13. Exemption from RIA step: assessment of the request

The oversight body assesses the exemption request. It must carefully review if the regulatory proposal really does not generate any cost to regulated parties. If so, it must issue the exemption approval. Otherwise, it must ask the ministry or government entity to prepare a RIA.

If the latter occurs, it would be advisable that the ministries or government entities begin the process of preparing the RIA in the step 3 of the moderate-impact RIA or high-impact RIA, taking into account that the first part of both processes is the same. After beginning the RIA process in step 3, the ministries or government entities could reassess the RIA process carried out so far, including a reassessment of costs.

As the steps listed below are the same as the ones for the high-impact/moderate-impact RIA, it is not necessary to repeat their description:

14. Sending to the CCV if applicable

15. Publication of the regulation

Figure 8.4. Suggested process to exempt from RIA regulations without compliance costs

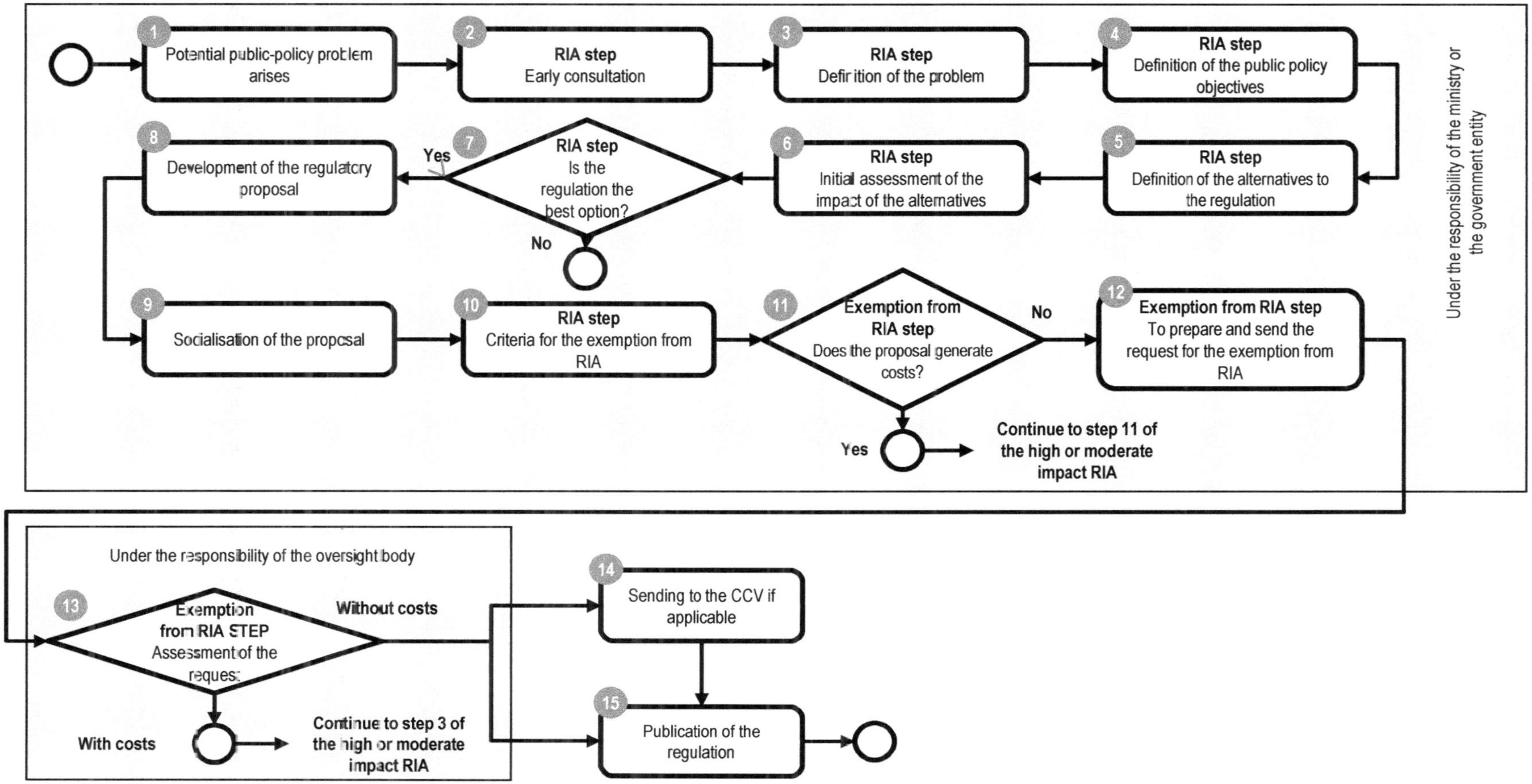

References

European Commission (2015), *Better Regulation Guidelines*, http://ec.europa.eu/smart-regulation/guidelines/docs/swd_br_guidelines_en.pdf (accessed on 26 April 2018). [1]

OECD (2016), *Regulatory Policy in Peru: Assembling the Framework for Regulatory Quality*, OECD Reviews of Regulatory Reform, OECD Publishing, Paris, https://dx.doi.org/10.1787/9789264260054-en. [3]

OECD (2015), *OECD Regulatory Policy Outlook 2015*, OECD Publishing, Paris, https://dx.doi.org/10.1787/9789264238770-en. [4]

OECD (2015), *Regulatory Policy in Perspective: A Reader's Companion to the OECD Regulatory Policy Outlook 2015*, OECD Publishing, Paris, https://dx.doi.org/10.1787/9789264241800-en. [2]

ORGANISATION FOR ECONOMIC CO-OPERATION AND DEVELOPMENT

The OECD is a unique forum where governments work together to address the economic, social and environmental challenges of globalisation. The OECD is also at the forefront of efforts to understand and to help governments respond to new developments and concerns, such as corporate governance, the information economy and the challenges of an ageing population. The Organisation provides a setting where governments can compare policy experiences, seek answers to common problems, identify good practice and work to co-ordinate domestic and international policies.

The OECD member countries are: Australia, Austria, Belgium, Canada, Chile, the Czech Republic, Denmark, Estonia, Finland, France, Germany, Greece, Hungary, Iceland, Ireland, Israel, Italy, Japan, Korea, Latvia, Lithuania, Luxembourg, Mexico, the Netherlands, New Zealand, Norway, Poland, Portugal, the Slovak Republic, Slovenia, Spain, Sweden, Switzerland, Turkey, the United Kingdom and the United States. The European Union takes part in the work of the OECD.

OECD Publishing disseminates widely the results of the Organisation's statistics gathering and research on economic, social and environmental issues, as well as the conventions, guidelines and standards agreed by its members.

OECD PUBLISHING, 2, rue André-Pascal, 75775 PARIS CEDEX 16
(42 2018 38 1 P) ISBN 978-92-64-30577-9 – 2019

www.ingramcontent.com/pod-product-compliance
Ingram Content Group UK Ltd.
Pitfield, Milton Keynes, MK11 3LW, UK
UKHW051504290926
15471UKWH00008B/1418

9 789264 305779